WORKING

A

DUCK

MELICIA PHILLIPS
AND
SEAN O. MCELROY

DOUBLEDAY

New York   London   Toronto   Sydney   Auckland

WORKING

A

DUCK

PUBLISHED BY DOUBLEDAY
a division of Bantam Doubleday Dell Publishing Group, Inc.
666 Fifth Avenue, New York, New York 10103

DOUBLEDAY and the portrayal of an anchor with a dolphin are
registered trademarks of Doubleday, a division of Bantam Doubleday
Dell Publishing Group, Inc.

Library of Congress Cataloging-in-Publication Data
Phillips, Melicia.
   Working a duck / by Melicia Phillips and Sean O. McElroy
      p.   cm.
   Includes bibliographical references and index.
   1. Cookery (Ducks)   I. McElroy, Sean O.   II. Title.
TX750.5.D82P45   1993
641.6′6597—dc20   92-5855
                                                          CIP

BOOK DESIGN AND ORNAMENTATION BY SIGNET M DESIGN, INC.

ISBN 0-385-42260-1

Printed in the United States of America
February 1993
9 8 7 6 5 4 3 2 1
FIRST EDITION

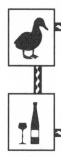

Acknowledgments

We would like to gratefully acknowledge all the friends and new acquaintances who aided us in the research and writing of this book. The culinary world at large owes a debt to all the dedicated breeders and farmers for their "behind-the-scenes" labor, but we are especially appreciative to them for opening their barndoors to us and providing information and anecdotes: Guillermo and Junny Gonzales of Sonoma Foie Gras, Claude Bigo of Grimaud Farms, Douglas Corwin of Crescent Duck Processing Co., Howard Josephs of Commonwealth Farms, Jim Reichart of Reichart Farms, Floyd Carter of Carter's Pheasant Farms, Cindy and John Lederer of Golden Crest Farm, Jack Klune, Andy Dunlop, and Elizabeth Coleman. There were chefs, wine personalities, and other generous people of the culinary world who aided us in bringing both new and traditional preparations of duck to our kitchens to experiment with: Karen and David Waltuck and Chanterelle, Ariane Daguin and George Faison of D'Artagnan, Kelvin and Nora Chu and Phoenix Garden, Jean-Louis Palladin and the staff of Jean-Louis at the Watergate, Brian McElroy, Michael Sullivan, Fran Fuller, David Fetherolf, Brian Mahony, Mark Hellerman of the New York Restaurant School, Charlie O'Donnell and Shawn Wines and Spirits, Matthew LaSorsa and Height's Chateau, Howard Kaplan and Executive Wine Seminars. In the area of literary advice and general moral support, we have been most privileged by those watching out for us: First, our "Redactrice en Chef" Judy Kern, Georgia Svolos (mother of Melicia Phillips), Tom LoPinto, John von Knorring, Barbara Goldman, Sabrina Buck, Matthew Shear, Mr. and Mrs. D. A. McElroy, Jean Fry, Rocky and Joe Gallo of United Meat Mkt., Joan Garvin, Mark Burns, Bernadette Vail, Karla Glasser, Paul Nuchims and family, Stinky Walrus, Jesus "Chewy" Trevino, Alice Keyser, Roger Dias, and Gregor Hall.

Lastly, we would like to dedicate this book to the memory of M. F. K. Fisher.

CONTENTS

Introduction

Consider the Sea Duck

The duck that migrates in the wild will always possess a stronger, gamier taste and tougher texture, which many people prefer to the more delicately flavored, commercially raised bird. Hunters know the importance of inspecting the stomach of a freshly killed bird to determine its diet and whether or not its meat is worth eating, for a duck feeding in grassy areas will render a sweeter meat. Wetlands are important to migratory fowl, but it is the smarter duck that migrates along coastal salt marshes. Once commonly referred to as sea duck, or the duck that no one wants to eat, this coastal bird is the ornithofication of wild gaminess. Coming from a harsher environment, this duck develops a tough, sinuous, and stringy flesh. It constantly eats saltwater fish, algae, little snails, gooey slugs, and a variety of tiny mollusks picked from the slimy black muck of the salt marshes. This diet renders the dark meat of sea duck pungent, astringent, and decidedly unpalatable. However, according to the recent discoveries of some food historians, sea duck was valued by many a lost mariner. Among the dangers these seamen faced was the potential for sailing into certain latitudes that were often prone to weak winds. These were the doldrums, and such a fate usually meant starvation for the sailor whose ship simply drifted aimlessly for months at a time. It was a mixed blessing when a sea duck alighted on one of these ships. It was welcomed as a sign that land was near, but its horrendous meat only teased the hunger of the desperate sailors.

The sea duck's fate seems to have changed when Antonio Dias, a Portugese ship builder and sea captain, discovered a way to feed his emaciated crew. His simple recipe included sacrificing a large piece of wood from the deck of his vessel, in this case French white oak, and boiling the wood with the sea duck for many hours. This allowed the oak to absorb some of the flavor and gaminess from the duck meat. The crew eagerly broke off pieces of the wood to munch on while quickly throwing the foul-smelling duck carcass overboard.

Who says he was a bold man that first ate an oyster?

▲ ▲ ▲

The average American kitchen is only just beginning to appreciate the delicious and versatile meat of the duck. Most of us approach duck with a great deal of apprehension and many misconceptions. We often think of it as exotic, intimidating, and strong-tasting. Americans who do appreciate duck usually eat it in restaurants and have rarely, if ever, prepared it at home. They might possibly have served a whole roasted duck for a special occasion but will never have explored the many uses that can make it an everyday food. Almost everyone views it as expensive, and probably the most popular misconception is that it is high in calories and very oily and fatty. Very often these perceptions are perpetuated by chefs who are equally unacquainted with duck, serving half a bird that was roasted well in advance, given a last-minute dunk in the deep fryer, and drenched with some sweet, sticky sauce.

Yet for certain cultures in America, such as Cajun and Asian, or in regions where ducks are hunted, there is a long tradition and appreciation for duck. Hunters will be familiar with the wild bird, which is leaner and tougher, and has a darker, gamier meat than the readily available Pekin duck. The Pekin gets its name from its Chinese origin and is not to be confused with "Peking Duck," which is a preparation (see page 138).

With few exceptions, most notably from James Beard, American cookbooks rarely offer duck recipes. Regional cookbooks of the South or Northwest are likely to offer a version of wild duck with a nice stuffing and a fruity glaze. While these are excellent means of preparation, there are countless other possibilities. Duck is not only one of the most delicious meats available, it is also one of the more versatile. It lends itself to many cooking techniques and styles, from braising to barbeque, from French and German to Thai and Chinese. It can serve as an elegant dinner-party centerpiece, or be transformed into a soup or salad or preserved as confit. It offers the highly prized culinary treasure of foie gras, the ever-intriguing duck tongue, and that formidable peasant sustenance food—duck feet.

There is now an increasing sophistication in the United States surrounding the versatility of this bird and the uses of all its parts. As this book will demonstrate, duck is for all seasons, lending itself to creative experimentation that borrows from an international mix of cuisines. Through such experimentation, you will discover how duck can be integrated into everyday meals in a surprisingly economical fashion. Taking the time to make stock, to render fat, and to make confit to have on hand will permit you to exercise your own creativity. Many of the recipes suggest ways of extending a duck and often require only minutes of preparation. For instance, the breasts may be filleted and sautéed rare, or at least less than well done, which gives the meat added savor and juiciness. They can be served up with a range of sauces and presented with quartered new potatoes roasted with duck fat and garlic. This leaves you with two good-sized legs, which you might roast or confit for future use in soups or salads. Trim the fat for a multiplicity of uses and save the carcass, neck, and wings for stocks, consommé, and sauces. The hearts and gizzards may also be used for confit and added to salads or served as hors d'oeuvres, and the livers can be sautéed or turned into mousse for an appetizer. Even the feet and tongue can be transformed into wonderful dishes. In the context of a full meal, one duck roasted whole, blatantly beautiful and succulent, with an unparalleled crispy skin, will easily feed a party of four. Two ducks purchased for an elegant dinner will yield four breasts for sautéing, will cost less than four portions of steak or lamb, and will still leave you with a refrigerator full of practical duck parts and by-products.

It is an unfortunate misconception that duck meat is strong flavored and oily. Ducks do have a healthy layer of fat beneath their skin, but the meat itself is quite lean (see Nutrition, page 10). For those seriously concerned about fat and calories, a skinless, sautéed breast of duck should pose no more problem than a breast of chicken. The properly prepared duck should have a crispy, golden brown skin with all or almost all the fat rendered off.

Different breeds of duck vary in their fat content and degree of gaminess. Mild Pekins are commonly available, but if a gamier character is desired, there are the Muscovy, Moulard, or Mallard ducks to choose from. All these ducks are produced commercially and have a meat that is full-bodied without the overwhelming gaminess of true wild duck.

This book is an exploration of food and wine. It will serve as a comprehensive survey of the cooking techniques and culinary styles appropriate for the various parts of the duck and for different breeds as well. We hope that, with this knowledge, you will make duck a more practical part of your culinary lifestyle and be able to experiment with it comfortably as an everyday food.

The wine commentary in this book is, in effect, situation specific. Its language is intended for the reader who possesses a basic knowledge of wine regions and an understanding of the compositional elements of wine. With such endless means of preparing duck, there are a variety of flavors from around the world that provide diverse and at times exotic combinations to complement its flavors and textures. The accepted tradition of matching a regional wine with cuisine of the same region is not always sufficient. Where appropriate, the classic matches of regional cooking have been perpetuated, but they are not intended to stand as hard-and-fast rules. For example, the pairing of roasted duck with a Burgundian Pinot Noir has centuries of tradition behind it but becomes an oversimplified solution for the complex mixture of flavors found in a Thai duck stew.

It is not our intention to radically redefine culinary traditions in headlong pursuit of a new dining trend, but rather to identify and use them as a starting point for creating interesting food and wine matches. There are certain food preparations that have for generations been associated with specific wines. For the most part these are dependable customs that have derived from earlier times when cooking was localized, or regional, as we might term it today. The development of both regional cuisine and wine making was determined by very definite natural forces. Vinification was passed along from generation to generation and subject to climate, soil type, and grape varietal. Likewise in culinary development, a region's natural resources determined certain methods of preparation and presentation. Somewhere in the midst of this there existed a symbiotic relationship of sorts between the kitchen and the winery. Consciously or not, taste sensations from one discipline influenced the other and subtle changes were made to accommodate their combined flavors. People of various regions knew their wine intimately, both as a part of their daily dining experience and as a cooking ingredient.

Today's consumer is faced with a much more worldwide perspective and a seemingly endless selection of well-made wines. Technological advances in vinicultural sciences have permitted regions throughout the world to become viable wine producers for international consumption. By the same token, many traditions in wine making have fallen victim to scientific advancements. More and more wine makers have succumbed to the economic demands of a global market so that many wines are no longer painstakingly vinified to suit the traditional cuisine of the region. Rather, production levels are increased, producing thinner wines vinified for early consumption, and fined and filtered to ensure safe passage to the palates of whichever country has the strongest currency at the time. Culinary arts are also moving to a new world beat, with many regions sharing each other's traditions. Diversification seems to be the way to go for many new restaurants, and increasing attention is being paid to dramatic changes in diet and eating habits. If wine is intended to be enjoyed with food, this leaves most consumers with few rules and a very haphazard approach to selection.

Without the luxury of a culinary tradition, we are required to find another means of marrying food and wine. Considering that no element of either the dish or the wine will go unaltered when the two are consumed together, a wine ought to be viewed almost as an additional ingredient in the preparation. Each recipe in this book is followed by a brief discussion of key ingredients and the compositional elements of various wines that might accompany the dish. Although the information given is directly related to each individual recipe, discovering why a combination works or fails will inevitably be useful in other dining situations. Certain adjectives applied to wine very often sound intimidating or meaningless. However, in time you will develop an improved sense of taste memory and begin to utilize the terminology for articulating taste interactions. You can refine the craft into what many might consider an art, and occasionally you will find wine that not only accompanies a recipe but elevates the meal to a higher, more sublime culinary experience.

Wine is a very complex topic, and this book does not intend to be authoritative or exhaustive in the information it provides. Suggestions are made to aid the taste memory and narrow down the range of possibilities. Wines are mentioned according to region and grape type, but more important, they are discussed in general terms according to their essential elements and how these will interact with the dominating influences of a particular recipe. No brand names or producers are included, and thus no rating is implied. Although there are important stylistic differences from producer to producer within a single region and grape type, these distinctions are discussed in other publications or can be learned from a wine merchant you trust. After reading the commentary in this book, you will be able to supply your merchant with a list of wine characteristics, utilizing some of the adjectives that have been provided. Rather than working with a list of specific producers or wine regions, you are provided with essential elements

that in some cases can be found in wines from many areas of the world. For instance, if you are looking for a crisp white wine without barrel fermentation to go with a delicate saffron sauce, you and your wine merchant will have many logical choices. Your knowledge and appreciation will be enhanced by more detailed and active participation. You'll acquire a sophistication that will allow you to make educated guesses and experiment with wines that have similar attributes but may not have been mentioned in this text. Using the general information in the wine commentary as a basic starting point, and understanding how the various elements of food and wine interact, will permit you to get adventurous and greatly enhance all your duck dishes.

HUSBANDRY

The commercial duck industry in the United States began about 1873 when the first Pekins were imported from China, where they had been domesticated for over a thousand years. There are colorful and conflicting stories about who imported these ducks and what happened to them. Originally, they may have been brought into San Francisco, where one dozen of them remained. The oldest duck farm in the country, Reichart Farms of Sonoma, California, established in 1901, claims to have the direct descendants of this original dynasty. The remaining few dozen ducks then made their way to the East Coast, brought either by an unknown entrepreneurial sea captain, by a certain Major Ashley of Britain, or possibly by James Rankin, a native of Boston.

An article published in 1910 in the *Reliable Poultry Journal* credits James Rankin with responsibility for the birth of the commercial duck industry by consciously creating a demand for ducks. Until that time, duck consumption was confined largely to hunters who shot their own, to farmers who raised a flock for sale locally, or to immigrants who were used to eating them in their native countries.

Before commercial breeding, ducks were small and did not have a good proportion of meat to bones, which made them uneconomical. There was a great difference in size between the sexes in some breeds and many had colored plummage that left the plucked ducks with dark pinfeathers, which were unattractive to the American consumer. Some breeds were neither consistent nor prodigious in their fertility, and for commercial purposes, the grower required a steady, reliable supply of new ducks. Consistency in size, appearance, and supply was necessary before a steady market could be found, especially in restaurants, where uniformity is important. Pekins were better market birds. They hatched in twenty-eight days (as compared, for example, to thirty-three days for the Muscovy); they grew to a good size, with very little difference between the ducks and drakes; their feathers and skin were creamy white; and they could be bred to yield a very good proportion of meat to bones. Perhaps as important, the Pekin had a mild-flavored meat, quite different from wild duck or even domesticated Muscovies, which gave it a broader appeal. Around the turn of the century, the ducks were still being fed a combination of grains, greens, and either fish or other protein meal to give them the wilder flavor they would have on their natural fish diet. However, as the industry developed, growers increased the popularity of their product by eliminating the fish meal altogether and further reducing the Pekin's gaminess. Today, farm-raised ducks are usually fed pellets containing grain and some kind of animal protein.

James Rankin encouraged the demand for his ducks by giving them away to hotels and wealthy families. This increased consumer interest in the bird and, together with his breeding techniques, created a market that by 1910 had produced almost 3 million birds. Duck farming in this early period was done on a much smaller scale than it is today, the majority of duck farms having production numbers in the thousands. The duck industry as a whole has expanded tremendously since its beginning and continues to grow. It has doubled since 1960, with almost 22 million ducks produced in 1989. This production, however, is carried out by fewer and fewer farms.

Historically, duck farming in the United States was centered in Suffolk county, New York, where it was a major industry. It thrived there on the eastern end of Long Island for a variety of geographic reasons, including a moderate climate, plenty of streams and ponds, and a proximity to the population centers of the East Coast. In addition, grain farming, already well established on the island, provided a steady, close food source.

At the peak of the industry on Long Island, there were over one hundred small farms, each producing a few thousand Pekins. Since duck farming was originally done mostly out of doors, it was a seasonal endeavor, shutting down in the depths of winter. It is only in the last twenty-five years that production has moved indoors and become a year-round industry.

The number of duck farms on Long Island has declined radically, from its peak of over one hundred, to sixty in the 1950s, twenty in 1986, and only six today producing about a million birds altogether. At one point, Long Island produced about 60 percent of the nation's Pekins, compared to less than 10 percent today. This is mainly because of the cost of doing business on the Island, as compared to the Midwest, where the other major producers are located. With feed accounting for approximately 60 percent of the cost of producing a duck, rising feed bills have had a serious impact on the industry. Compounded by very high energy rates and inflation in general, this makes it difficult for a small farmer to stay in business. Expanding is nearly impossible since real estate values on the eastern end of Long Island have skyrocketed to $100,000 or more per acre. Many farmers just saw more sense in selling their land than in trying to make a living at duck farming. This in turn has brought more development to the area, further encroaching on the rural environment conducive to farming.

The duck farms remaining on Long Island stay in business by competing with the larger processors in the area of quality. The Midwestern growers take advantage of lower labor, land, and energy costs to grow greater quantities of birds, with the largest producer processing about 10 million a year. While the ducks from these farms are all of good quality, the Long Island duck is superior. The Long Island farmers realize that they cannot compete on price, so they offer a duck that surpasses those of the larger producers in both appearance and flavor. This is done by complicated genetic breeding, specialized feed mixes, and more costly and careful processing. All this, combined with the factors discussed above, increases the cost of the final product by about fifteen cents per pound, or seventy-five cents per five-pound duck.

These same facts hold true for the smaller producers on the West Coast, where both old and newly established boutique duck farms cater to high-quality restaurants. The Chinese populations of both coasts also demand a high-quality duck to prepare many of their specialties, and it is this market, combined with fine dining establishments, that sustains these producers.

Today, the Long Island duckling is still associated with quality, so much so that other producers often misrepresent their product as Long Island grown by using Long Island addresses or geographical names on their labels. In some cases the birds are raised elsewhere and finished or processed on Long Island and then labeled as Long Island duckling. More innocently, the history of the Pekin in the United States is so strongly associated with Long Island that the term "Long Island duckling" is often mistaken for a breed itself, regardless of the duck's origin. The genuine Long Island duck, completely raised, bred, and processed there, will bear only the label of either the Crescent or the South Shore producers, and these are distributed mainly to restaurants. See Sources, page 179.

▲　▲　▲

There are five breeds of duck grown for meat in the United States: Pekin, Muscovy, Moulard, Mallard, and Rouen. Of these, the Pekin, with its creamy white feathers, is by far the most popular. This bird is prized for its plump breast meat and for its skin, which, when roasted, becomes a thin, golden brown, crispy, crackling shell around the moist meat. The Pekin is bred and fed to have a mild meat, entirely different from that of wild duck. Within this breed, however, there can be a range of gaminess, depending on decisions made by the grower. Pekins are raised on large farms, which are really just a collection of long, barnlike structures that house the ducks. Because ducks are hardy birds and fairly resistant to disease, most duck farmers make claims to raising their ducks naturally, without hormones or antibiotics and in open housed areas rather than in isolated cages such as those used to breed commercial chickens. Housing is important to the growers because it isolates their ducks from wild ones that may carry disease, cuts down drastically on feed bills, and allows them to produce year round. The ducks need no water to swim in and are actually kept away from any water that might wet them and produce a chill. Believe it or not, duck farmers worry about drowning ducks, and this is especially true for the young ducklings.

The eggs of the Pekin are hatched in twenty-eight days and the ducks are raised for anywhere from thirty-eight to fifty days, at which time they should weigh about seven pounds and their meat has matured. They are not grown any larger because this is a good table size and, probably more important, because their growth rate slows down considerably at this point and it is not economical to feed them anymore.

Most Pekins are processed as whole, dressed birds, which means they have been eviscerated, with the head and feet removed. The United States Department of Agriculture does not consider the head and feet edible, but some communities, most notably the Buddhists, insist that they be left on. According to Buddhist theory, this is done out of respect for the animal—it needs its feet to walk through heaven and its head to see where it is going. A processor may obtain what is known as a Buddhist exemption and thereby process the ducks this way. He may also get a Confucian exemption, which allows him to sell the ducks plucked but completely uneviscerated. This is sometimes also known as a New York dress. The best place to find a duck dressed in one of these ways is in Chinatown shops.

Processing is done by a combination of computer-operated machinery and human labor. After slaughter, the ducks are bled and then moved throughout the processing plant on an overhead conveyor. The first stop is plucking. The ducks are first dipped in hot water and then mechanically plucked. The feathers are then washed, dried, and packed into bales for shipping. They are sold to manufacturers of down products and provide the duck grower with a significant part of his income. After plucking, the duck is dipped in hot wax to remove its pinfeathers. Some of the more careful producers will repeat the waxing stage and maybe even tweeze the ducks. The duck is then sent around the plant, with different parts of the bird removed at each station. The tongues and feet are mostly exported, as are the carcasses (when the ducks are prepared as boneless breasts and legs), and the heads. Every processed duck must undergo a USDA inspection, which is done to assure the consumer that the meat is free of disease. (There are exceptions to this rule, depending on who you sell to and in what volume.) The duck can then be graded, although this is not mandatory and is done by a state employee according to federal regulations at the cost of the producer. A duck is lowered a grade for pinfeathers, broken limbs, torn skin, bruises, and the like. These lower-grade birds are usually sold at a lower price to the food service trade and are used as parts for preparations such as pâtés, where appearance is not important. The ducks are processed both as whole, dressed birds and as parts such as boneless breasts and legs, which are becoming more widely available. They are then sorted for size and packaged. At the larger houses, the majority of the ducks are then frozen, either for overseas sales or because of a lag in consumer demand. The smaller producers have a higher percentage of fresh product, or do a complete business in fresh ducks.

The consumer will find some variation among the different brands on the market. Growers decide what their product goals are—to produce a bird with less fat, more breast meat, or more flavor ("a duckier duck")—and they control these factors through breeding and feed.

The Muscovy duck is native to South America, where it was first domesticated. The only variety not to descend from the Mallard, the Muscovy is an unusual-looking duck. It can be white or of various colors, its most distinguishing features being the red caruncles on its face and its lack of quack. It makes more of a hissing sound. (In general, ducks tend to be louder than drakes in all varieties.) Given the opportunity, Muscovies will roost in trees and have a clawed foot suitable for this purpose.

While the Muscovy is one of the hardier ducks and has good fertility, it has taken a backseat to the Pekin in terms of commercial production, probably because of the substantial difference in size and maturation time between the sexes. The duck takes ten weeks to mature to four pounds dressed, while the drake takes twelve weeks to mature and is six to seven pounds dressed.

Muscovies are leaner than Pekins, possibly because they originated in warmer South American climates and did not require as much insulating fat. According to a major producer, the skinless breast is 98 percent fat free, making it one of the leanest meats available (see page 10 for more on nutrition).

In France, where duck consumption is many times what it is here, the vast majority of the ducks eaten are Muscovies, with the rest made up mostly of Moulards, Rouens, and a few esoteric varieties. The Pekin, so popular in the United States, is virtually unavailable in France.

Compared to the Pekin, the Muscovy is noted for its redder meat and gamier flavor. The breasts of both sexes are quite plump with deep flavor, which makes them ideal for sautéing. The smaller female is fine for roasting or preparing in any way you would a Pekin, but although it will crisp, it will not result in the beautiful crackling skin required for a Peking Duck because of the lower fat content. While the Muscovy drake breasts are fine for sautéing, the legs do tend to be a little tough. They can be enjoyed roasted, but a better preparation would be as a confit or stew —something that would increase their tenderness. They are actually preferred for this kind of dish, especially confit, because of their hardy taste and good size, and because they tend to fall apart less than the more tender breeds.

Muscovy ducks are not as readily available as Pekins. They are mostly seen in restaurants, although they can be bought through specialty meat shops, directly from purveyors, or from the farms themselves (see page 179 for sources).

Perhaps the most interesting aspect of the Muscovy is its complicity in the production of foie gras. Muscovies themselves are used to produce foie gras and the males are also bred with the female Pekin to produce the Moulard. (see page 8 for more on foie gras).

▲ ▲ ▲

The Moulard is a very large duck, weighing seven to eight pounds dressed, with a combination of white and black feathers. It is also sometimes known as the mule duck, because it is a sterile crossbreed. Its prime characteristic is its liver, which is ideal for the production of foie gras. Although commonly misused in this country, the French term *magret* refers to the breast meat of the fattened Moulard duck. The breast is quite large, weighing about two pounds, and can easily serve four. The Moulard has a stronger-flavored meat than the Pekin, Rouen, or Muscovy duck, and is somewhat richer because of the fattening process used to produce foie gras. In recent years, Moulard meat has become somewhat milder, perhaps in an effort to popularize it.

To increase its tenderness, the meat is often aged on the bone for seven days prior to marketing, but it is still chewier than that of the other ducks and it is for this reason, together with its gaminess, that special care must be taken in its preparation. Sautéing or grilling can be a fine way to cook it, especially the magrets from smaller birds, but the meat may be rendered more tender by preparing it as cutlets or by moist cooking methods such as braising. Confit, of course, remains an excellent technique. The assertive meat pairs well with many strongly flavored sauces and garnishes that would overwhelm the milder ducks. The skin of the breast is relatively thick, and although with careful cooking you can serve the breast with skin intact, it is better to remove it. It makes excellent cracklings as well as providing you with a good amount of rendered fat. As for the Moulard legs, the best way to cook them is as a stew or confit. Roasting simply toughens them.

▲ ▲ ▲

The Mallard is a small duck with colorful feathers, weighing between two and one-half to three pounds dressed, and is the duck from which all others except the Muscovy descend. It is believed to have been first domesticated in China over a thousand years ago. As it exists in the wild, it has a gamy, almost fishy taste, and is also quite lean and therefore suffers considerably from freezing. One can understand why older cookbooks commonly call for moist heat cooking methods such as boiling or braising, as the duck is too small and lean to benefit from roasting. The breeding of Mallards is not nearly as widespread or large scale as the breeding of Pekins, so the product is subject to a great deal of variation and can therefore be unreliable, expensive, and seasonal. You will most likely find fresh Mallards between fall and late winter or early spring Should you find a reliable source of Mallards fed specifically for the table, through a distributor, at a specialty shop, or directly from a producer, don't hesitate to take advantage of it. Mallard meat is very lean with a silky texture and is quite beeflike and juicy when properly cooked. The breasts are perfect for sautéing and the skin is lean enough to eliminate the extra step of rendering the fat (see page 28). The legs are small and are best braised to serve alongside the breasts.

▲ ▲ ▲

The Rouen duck is a French breed, known for its thin skin and very mild meat. Although the Rouen yields a good proportion of meat to bones and is grown to about four to four and one-half pounds dressed, its dark feathers and lower egg production have kept it from becoming more of a presence in the American marketplace. In the United States it is grown primarily by small producers for fine dining establishments and specialty shops, particularly on the West Coast. The Rouen is much more popular in France, especially in Normandy, where the town for which it was named is located. Because the Rouen is more expensive to raise, it is primarily used in France for pressed duck, a specialty often called duck Rouennais. Traditionally, the duck for this dish is smothered, which keeps the blood in the meat and enriches its normally mild character, as well as providing plenty of juices for the sauce.

Foie Gras

The secret of foie gras dates back to ancient Rome, where geese are said to have been fattened with figs and honey. Foie gras is the fattened liver of either duck or goose, although for the purposes of this book we will discuss only duck foie gras. Being migratory waterfowl, ducks have a natural capacity to store fat in their liver. In the wild, the duck will gorge itself to create an energy reserve before migration. To create the same effect in a commercial situation, the birds are force-fed in the last few weeks before they are sent to market. (Exactly what they are fed is a jealously guarded secret, although a grain mixture with a corn base is certain.) This special fattening procedure is a physiological process, not a pathological one. That is, it does not produce a diseased, damaged, or unnatural liver—in fact, the process is reversible. The foie gras producer, therefore, utilizes the built-in characteristics of the duck, creating a liver that has grown to about eight times its original weight.

This method is not regulated in the United States; however, the producer logically wants to treat his birds well in order to achieve a high-quality product. A stressed duck is more susceptible to disease, does not put on as much weight, becomes belligerent, and does not produce as nice a meat.

Foie gras is produced in quite a few countries including France, Hungary, Israel, and Canada. The French are, without doubt, most famous for their foie gras although, according to an industry source, 80 percent of the foie gras now sold in France actually comes from Hungary, Poland, or Israel. If the final processing is done in France, it can then be labeled a product of France. In the United States, commercial production of domestic foie gras began in 1982, and there are now a handful of foie gras–producing farmers in this country. Prior to domestic production, all foie gras was imported and, by federal regulation, had to be cooked before it could be brought in. This meant the fresh, uncooked liver was not available, although canned foie gras, foie gras products, or demi-cuit (literally half-cooked) livers were.

The two breeds of duck that are used to produce foie gras in the United States are the Moulard and the Muscovy. There are a few differences between the foie gras of these ducks. Whereas either the male or the female Moulard is suitable for foie gras production, only the Muscovy drake is used because of its larger size and because the liver of the female tends to be too veiny. The most significant difference between these birds' foie gras is in the cooking. While both are equal in flavor, the Moulard holds on to its fat better and does not shrink as much in the preparation. At least 90 percent of foie gras in the United States is sold in restaurants. It is an expensive product, although prices have recently dropped significantly because of an increase in producers. However, a little goes a long way—a one-pound foie gras can easily yield ten portions as an appetizer. Its sheer deliciousness—delicate liver flavors highlighted and sweetened by the extra-silky fat—make it impossible to resist. A properly prepared foie gras can leave you with a sensuous culinary memory that will last a lifetime.

The producer will judge his livers to be grade A, B, or C. A high-quality, grade A liver should be of good size (about 1¼ pounds), have a firm texture, and be of clear yellowish-beige color without any bloodiness or excessive veining. While a liver may be downgraded on these points, a foie gras of a lesser grade is also much less expensive and may be perfectly fine for many preparations. Grade A foie gras is most appropriate for use in terrines and pâtés where appearance is of great importance. Grade B can sometimes be used for terrines, especially if it has only been downgraded for size, but is most useful for sautéing or roasting, or for mousses. The grade C liver is usually suitable only for mousses or stuffings.

Foie gras is often served during the winter holiday season. This is because the ducks and geese were traditionally force-fed in the fall when the weather turned cooler. By the time the holidays came, the ducks and geese would be ready with their own contribution to the festivities.

Nutrition

It is a popular misconception that duck is a fatty meat. Actually, the majority of duck fat is contained in the skin. The meat itself is quite lean, although different breeds of duck will vary in their fat content, and even the same breed will vary between producers, depending on breeding and feed. A Pekin duck breast, boneless and skinless and weighing 3.5 ounces, has 170 calories, 29.6 grams of protein, 2.2 mg of iron, 7.28 mg of niacin, 4.9 g fat, and 160 mg of cholesterol.[*] The fat is 78 percent monounsaturated. Other breeds such as the Muscovy and the Rouen are even leaner, with the Muscovy breast about 98 percent fat-free. Of course, a lot of the fun of eating duck is in the skin, but most of the fat in duck skin can and should be rendered during

---

[*] Information provided by Concord Farms.

cooking. The point is that properly prepared duck is not greasy or fatty and is nutritionally comparable to other meats.

There is an interesting new theory regarding duck fat and meat. It is based on the fact that France has the second lowest rate of heart disease in the industrialized world, half of that in the United States, even though they consume four times as much butter and twice as much cheese and lard as Americans. More interestingly, the lowest rate of heart disease in France is in the Gascony region—precisely where the cuisine is based on duck and goose and where the fats from these birds are used for cooking and eating. The answer might lie in wine and copper. Duck, geese, and organ meats, which are popular in Gascony, are high in copper. The French also have a higher wine consumption than Americans. It seems that copper is what the body needs to handle fat and cholesterol and that wine helps the body absorb copper from foods. It is also important to note that duck fat has half the cholesterol of butter, which makes it a great idea for spreading on bread, making croutons, and sautéing. Currently, a study of what is being termed "The French Paradox" is being conducted by French and American scientists and is expected to take several years.

A Growth Industry

In 1873 a small number of Pekin ducks were imported to the United States by James Rankin, who started the duck industry and witnessed its growth to several million birds raised annually by the turn of the century. We wish that Mr. Rankin were here today to share with us some stories involving the sexuality of ducks. Visiting several duck farms, we witnessed the almost comical lack of sexual restraint among drakes. It makes one wonder how rabbits possibly got their reputation.

Where humans are concerned, drakes are great bonders—ask any of the farmers experimenting with artificial insemination. If one person should take a vacation and leave a stranger behind to rub the drake's belly, there will be an indignant lack of response. On one farm, we witnessed a most sorrowful sight when the owner showed us the wing of his barn that was reserved for his Muscovy misfits. Here we saw the poor fellows mounting, falling off, remounting the same duck and falling off again, over and over without success, until the female waddled away in disgust. They were waiting to be sold to local parks and private ponds for a dollar a piece.

The strangest account was given by a woman from New York State who was awakened in the middle of the night by her flock of Pekins. When she shined a light on the strange sounds that drew her outside, she discovered a pyramid many feet high. She stood watching for quite some time but could not figure out what had provoked the copulating frenzy that resulted in several smothered birds. Let us be thankful that this species never discovered the amorous effects of too much wine.

BUTCHERING AND CARVING

A Note on Butchering

While the directions given here for butchering are lengthy and detailed, butchering is really not difficult. You can't go too far wrong if you keep a few things in mind. First, a sharp knife is essential. Always work with the tip of the knife, keeping it pointed downward. When boning, just stay close to the bones, and take your time until you are more comfortable and familiar with the physiology of the duck. When removing legs and wings, always cut through the joints, never through bone. When you are unsure of what to do, let the duck itself guide you. All birds have lines of fat where their joints are, showing you where to cut if you want to separate them. The duck will actually come apart quite easily. All you are doing for the most part is guiding the knife through the natural separations in the body.

To Butterfly, Halve, and Quarter a Duck

1   Trim excess fat from the cavity and neck of the duck. Set the duck with its back to you in a sitting position.

2   With a sharp cleaver, start chopping down either side of the neck, along the backbone, cutting a couple of inches down on one side, then the other. Continue cutting, alternating along either side of the backbone, past the shoulderblades, and through the joint where the leg is attached to the body, until the backbone is free. Reserve the backbone for stock.

3   Remove the first two joints of the wing and reserve them for stock.

4   Place the duck flat, skin side down. Make a small incision at the top of the breastbone to expose it. Run your finger down along either side of the breastbone and the soft cartilage beneath it, separating it from the meat. Pull out the breastbone and reserve it for stock. You now have a butterflied duck.

5   Cut the duck in half, following the line left by the breastbone. You now have two half ducks.

6   To quarter the duck, place it skin side up. Gently pull the breast quarter and leg quarter in opposite directions to separate them and cut in between. You now have a quartered duck with the bone in.

To Quarter a Duck with Boneless Breasts

1   Place the duck, breast side up, with the cavity facing you. Gently pull the legs toward you, pushing your fingers in between each leg and the body. This will enable you to make an incision without cutting into the breast.

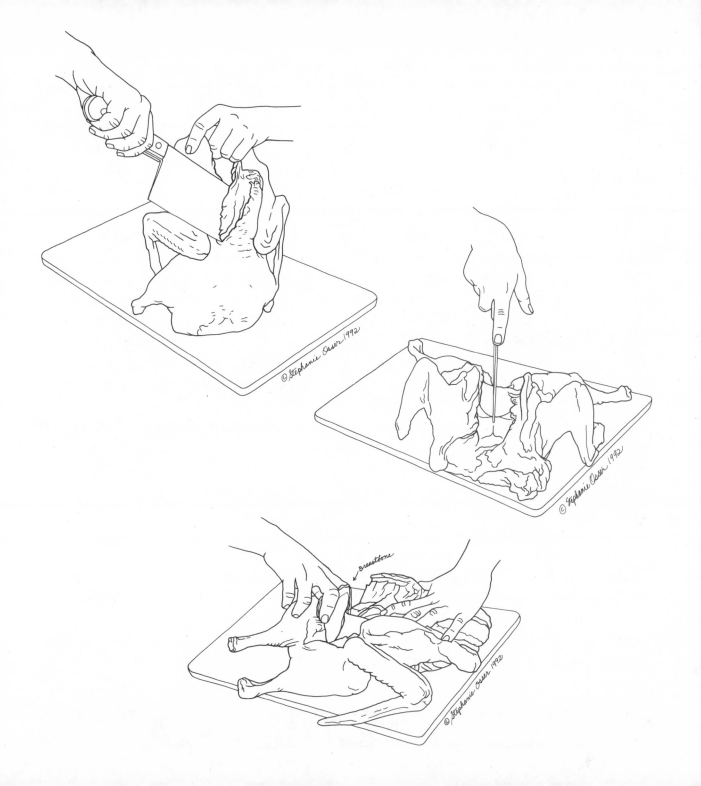

Breastbone

2   Remove the legs one at a time by making an incision between the leg and body, starting at the point where the leg meets the thigh. Cut as close to the body as possible, without taking skin away from the breast, so you have enough skin to cover the leg meat.

3   Turn the duck on its breast. Cut around the leg, straight to the backbone. Pop the leg joint out of its socket by bending the leg backward. Cut in between the joint and sever the leg, keeping close to the backbone. Repeat with the other leg.

4   Place the bird breast side up, with the cavity facing you. With the tip of your knife, cut along either side of the breastbone, keeping very close to it. Turn the duck around, placing it with the neck facing you. Cut around the wishbone, tipping your knife so that you are actually cutting the meat away from under the bone as much as you can. With your finger, gently separate the meat from the breastbone along your incision. Turn the duck around again, so that the cavity is facing you. With the tip of your knife, carefully cut the breast away from the carcass, gently pulling it with your hand as you go. The meat will come away quite easily—you are only helping it along with light strokes of your knife. Repeat with the other side of the breast.

5   Place the breast filets skin side down on the board. Remove any obvious veins. With the palm of your hand, smack the skin near the neck side of the breast to flatten it somewhat. Trim the excess skin from the breast, but not very closely, as it will shrink when cooked. If you are cooking the breast with the skin on, score the skin by making crosshatched cuts, but do not cut all the way through to the meat.

6   To remove the skin, keep the breast on the board, skin side down. Starting at the neck end, separate the skin from the meat a little, lifting up the meat somewhat. Hold your knife perpendicular to the skin, starting where you have lifted the meat. Pulling the skin in the opposite direction from which you are cutting, use a light and gentle back and forth scraping motion to separate the meat and skin. You are not cutting the meat or skin, but releasing the delicate connective tissue. Reserve the skin for cracklings and rendered fat (see page 26).

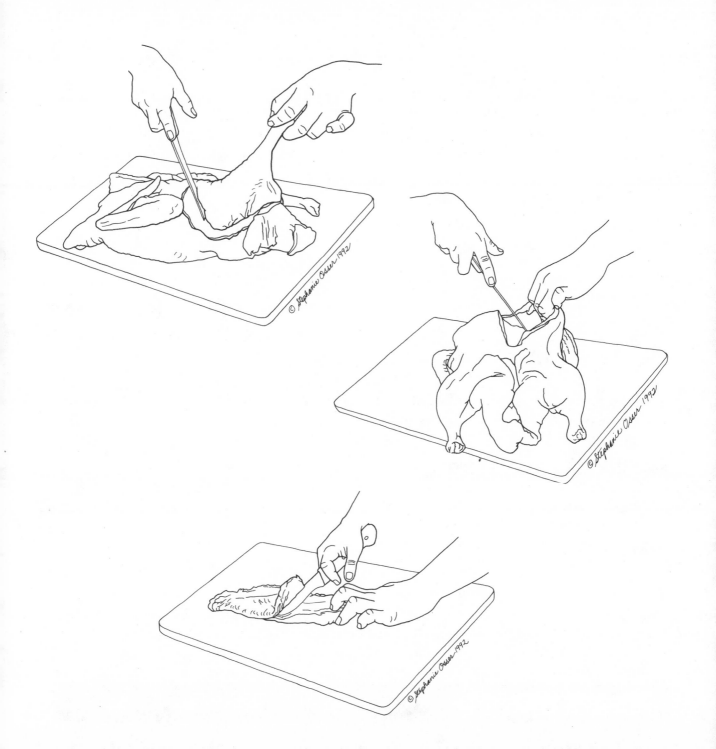

Two Ways to Bone a Whole Duck

Using the first method, you end up with a boned duck that can be opened out flat. For a ballottine, in which you want to create even layers of different stuffings or designs, this gives you better control. The duck is then tied up into its original shape.

In the second method, the skin is not cut through at all. This is better when you are using a stuffing that can be pushed into the duck. The duck's original shape is filled out with the stuffing and only the cavity end needs to be trussed.

METHOD ONE

1   Place the duck on its back on a board with the cavity facing you. Remove the wings at the second joint and reserve them for stock. Make incisions circling the ankles and the ends of the wings, cutting through the skin and severing the tendons.

2   Place the bird on its breast. Make an incision along the backbone. Start carefully scraping the duck meat away from the carcass on one side, starting at the neck and moving down toward the tail. When you get to the hip joint, pop the leg out of its socket and continue scraping away the duck meat from the main carcass, keeping the leg with the rest of the meat.

3   When you reach the breastbone, repeat the process on the other side. Be very careful when you reach the breastbone—the skin is directly attached to the cartilage and can be easily punctured.

4   Once you have totally freed the duck of its carcass, except where it is attached to the breastbone, lift the carcass up slightly, so the duck meat is hanging down. This will give you a better view and easier access. Carefully cut along the breastbone to totally separate the carcass. Reserve the bones for stock.

5   Place the duck skin side down on the board. Beginning at the thigh bone, scrape the meat away from the bone until you reach the ankle. Pull out the leg bone and reserve it for stock. Repeat with the other leg and with the wings as well.

6   Trim away any excess fat, veins, or cartilage.

METHOD TWO

1   Place the duck on its back with the neck facing you. With the tip of your boning knife, cut around the wishbone and remove it. Reserve for another use.

2   Turn the duck on its breast, and beginning at the top of the backbone, start carefully scraping the skin from the bone. Work your way around the bird, toward the breastbone, keeping your knife between the flesh and bone and never puncturing the skin.

3   Turn the duck over as you need to, to make the process more comfortable. Continue scraping the meat away from the carcass, going about halfway into the bird. Pop the wing joints and cut between them and the main carcass.

4   Turn the duck around so that the cavity is facing you. Continue separating the meat from the bone, going around the bird. Pop the leg joints and cut between them and the main carcass. Once you have freed the carcass, remove it from the duck and reserve it for another use.

5   Carefully turn the duck inside out. Scrape the meat away on both thigh bones and cut through the drumstick and thigh joint. Remove the thigh bones and reserve for another use. Repeat the process with the first wing bone.

6   Remove any excess fat from the inside of the duck. Remove any veins, cartilage, or large tendons. Turn the duck right side out.

Carving the Duck

1   After the duck has roasted, let it rest for five minutes. If the duck has been stuffed, remove the stuffing.

2   Place the duck with the cavity facing you, and with a carving or boning knife, remove the legs first. Hold on to the duck with the flat side of your carving fork, being careful not to puncture the skin. Cut around the legs, probing into the thigh joint with the tip of your knife to pop the leg out. Cut straight down to free the leg. If desired, you may separate the thigh and drumstick by laying the leg upside down and cutting through the joint where you see a line of fat.

3   Slice the breast. Cut diagonally, starting at the area over the wing joint, and carve the meat into thin slices with a piece of skin attached to each.

THE SPINSTERS OF LUPPE-VIOLLES

If you possess sound teeth, a nimble tongue, and the fierce heart of a devout carnivore, a demoiselle contest is something that you ought not to miss. The term "demoiselle" has curious literal translations concerning the unmarried woman, but proper understanding of the term might necessitate a trip to the heart of Gascony. In the small town of Luppe-violles, duck is consumed faster than its carcasses can be simmered into stock and the locals have gone to great lengths to see that every part of the duck is fully utilized. The backbone and ribs, with bits of meat remaining, are grilled and then termed a "demoiselle." Unlike the American pie-eating contest, which is based on quantity of consumption, here the objective is to clean the demoiselle as thoroughly as possible in an allotted time. The people of Luppe-violles hold their annual demoiselle-eating contest in midsummer, drawing international competitors, many of whom arrive costumed in traditional Gascon dress. First place is determined by the barest bones, judged by a group of locals (who may also be swayed by creative costuming). If you suspect you might do well in such an event, you might consider that the greater your appreciation for Gascon cuisine, the dearer first prize is likely to be. The winner is allowed to step onto a scale, which is then balanced out with an equal weight of wine from the local vineyards.

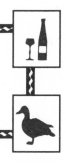

BASICS

How to Cook a Duck Breast

A wide variety of techniques may be used to cook duck, producing different results in the way of texture and doneness. When it is roasted as a whole bird, all the meat must by necessity be cooked to well done if you are to produce a gorgeously browned and crisped duck. The meat remains delicious and moist, however, because it gets constant basting from the rendering fat, and roasting it on the bone gives it extra flavor.

When you are sautéing the breast alone, it is better to cook it as rare as you can take it because it is juicier and more tender this way. Duck breast is delicious seared in a very hot pan and left blood rare, with the meat just warmed through in the center. While this may not be to everyone's taste, certainly medium-rare to medium should not be too radical for most palates. (While people have been eating duck this way for many years, the USDA does not recommend the eating of rare duck or other rare or raw meats because of possible salmonella poisoning.) The trick is to produce a sautéed duck breast with rare meat and a crispy skin. This is easily accomplished by a slow rendering of the fat.

First, heat a skillet until very hot. You will know the pan is hot enough when a drop of water evaporates immediately on contact. It must be hot enough for the fat to instantly begin to melt out of the skin—no added oil is necessary. Place a boneless duck breast skin side down in the hot skillet. Immediately reduce the flame to medium-low. The flame should not be hot enough to cook the meat, just to render the fat. Leave the duck breast in the pan, occasionally pouring off the fat and reserving it for another use, for about fifteen minutes. The skin will be nicely browned and the meat will still be completely raw. This may be done a day in advance of

final cooking. It is best to chill the breast in any case, if you are going to have it less than well done, as it cooks better that way.

When you are ready to serve, heat some oil or duck fat in a skillet until the fat just begins to smoke. Add the duck breast skin side down, lower the flame to medium-hot, and sauté until the skin is well crisped. Turn the duck breast over and sauté the other side. It is difficult to give exact timing for the degrees of doneness because cooking times will vary according to the size, breed, and fat content of your duck. The best way to tell would be to poke the thicker end, under the tenderloin, with your finger. This is the point where the breast cooks last. Experience will tell you when it is cooked to your liking—the springier the meat feels, the more it is cooked. The leaner the meat, the quicker it will cook—ranging from about four minutes total for rare to six minutes for well done when dealing with a Pekin or Muscovy. When it has reached the desired doneness, remove it from the pan and let it rest for one minute. Slice lengthwise into five or six slices for a fanned presentation.

To cook a skinless duck breast, remove the skin according to the directions on page 15 and sauté it, turning once, in a very hot pan with some duck fat or olive oil.

Another alternative is to cook the duck meat and skin separately, sautéing the breast and broiling the skin, then cutting the skin into strips to use as garnish for the meat.

A favorite way to prepare duck is to roast the leg separately and serve it with the rare sautéed breast, garnished with any of the sauces in the next chapter. Each component is thereby cooked according to its own needs, providing variety and contrast in taste and texture.

Roasting Duck

There is more than one way to roast a duck. The recipes in this book vary in their techniques as well as cooking times and temperatures. In general, slower roasting gives more time for the fat in the skin to render, leaving the skin crisper and less fatty, which is, of course, essential to Peking Duck. The gentler heat also produces more tender meat. One trick is to tie the cavity closed to seal in the juices, thus steaming the duck from the inside as the outside roasts. Paul Prudhomme takes the slow method to the extreme, cooking a duck in a very slow oven for about five hours.

A quicker cooking is fine, too, and will result in a wonderful roasted Pekin in about 1¼ hours. The use of an adjustable wire roasting rack will enable you to raise the duck above the rendered fat and drippings, cooking the duck more evenly with a crisp dry skin.

Stock and Demi-Glace

The preparation of a good, flavorful, gelatinous stock is essential for all soups, stews, and sauces. In addition to providing liquid as a cooking medium, stock contributes necessary flavor and gelatin. It is the gelatin that adds body and viscosity to the finished dish or sauce. A well-structured stock is especially obvious in consommés, which are reduced and clarified stocks, usually with little seasoning.

For the purposes of this book, the term "demi-glace" refers to a stock that has been reduced by half. It is used in recipes where a quicker preparation is desired.

Duck Stock

2 duck carcasses
1 small carrot, cut into
½-inch slices
1 onion, skin left on, cut into
8 pieces
1 bay leaf
pinch of thyme
5 whole black peppercorns

*S*tock may be made with the carcasses of the duck after it has been boned, as well as any necks, wing tips, feet, or gizzards you have. The bones should always be roasted to make a brown stock with a beautiful amber color. You may also use the carcass of a roasted duck after carving, provided it has not been stuffed.

1   Place the carcasses on a sheet pan and roast in a 450° oven until nicely browned, about 45 minutes.

2   With a cleaver, chop the bones a bit to make them fit more easily in a pot.

3   Add the rest of the ingredients to the pot with the carcasses and cover with cold water. Bring to a boil, reduce to a simmer, and cook for 4 hours. You should skim the stock occasionally and add additional water to keep the bones covered if necessary. Duck bones tend to float, so they will always be sticking out of the water somewhat.

4   Strain the stock through a sieve and cool before refrigerating.

5   The stock will keep in the refrigerator for at least a week, maybe longer. To extend its shelf life, bring the stock to a boil every few days. If keeping longer than a week, however, it is best to freeze it and defrost it when needed. It can also be reduced to demi-glace before freezing if space is a concern. Once refrigerated, the fat will rise to the top and solidify, making it easy to remove.

Basic Duck Aspic

1 Bring the consommé to a boil. Add salt to taste.

2 Place the gelatin in a bowl. Add 3 tablespoons of cold water, stir to combine, and let sit for 3 minutes. Add the hot consommé to this and stir to dissolve the gelatin completely.

3 Proceed with your recipe.

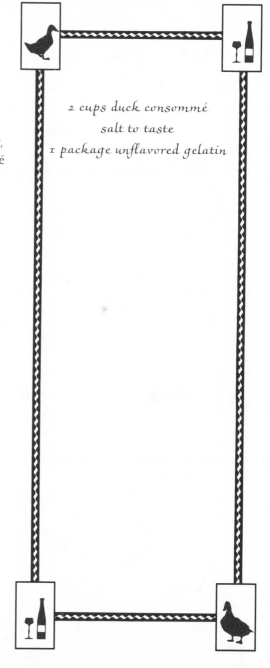

2 cups duck consommé
salt to taste
1 package unflavored gelatin

How to Clean a Foie Gras

1   Let the foie gras come to room temperature to facilitate the removal of the veins.

2   Gently separate the lobes of the liver. Using a kitchen towel for a better grip, lightly tug on the large, visible veins, which should come out. If there is some resistance or if the vein breaks, be careful not to force it to the point of damaging the foie gras.

3   Sometimes you can peel off the very thin membrane on the surface of the liver, using the kitchen towel again for your grip. Other times the membrane will be too delicate to grab.

4   Chill the foie gras before cooking.

Rendering Duck Fat

Duck fat is not a waste product, but a valuable by-product of the duck. Most of the fat is in a layer beneath the skin, where it serves to provide the insulation necessary for waterfowl. Luckily, this allows for easy removal and rendering. To make the duck more delicious and healthful, it is necessary to render as much of this fat as possible and still leave the lean meat moist and cooked to the proper degree of doneness. To maintain its usefulness, collect the fat periodically as it cooks off to keep it from browning. Stored well wrapped in the refrigerator, the fat can then be saved for a variety of other purposes.

Rendering the fat from trimmed duck skin yields a prized by-product—cracklings. The skin is cut up into small pieces which are slowly cooked until the fat has melted out of them and they are left as crispy morsels. These can be used in salads, as a garnish, or baked into bread or biscuits.

A store of rendered duck fat is as good as money in the bank and should be continuously replenished. Rendered fat is indispensable for preparing and preserving confits (see page 121) and rillettes (see page 66). It is exciting to add variety to a meal by scooping out a tablespoon to use for frying potatoes and onions, or even fish, instead of the usual vegetable or olive oil. With only half the cholesterol of butter, it can also be flavored and used as a spread for bread (see page 173 for more on the nutritive value of duck fat). You may even find yourself becoming unexpectedly fond of your crock of fat, and saddened to see it diminish as it is consumed. You'll be faced with life's dilemma of wanting to eat it, yet wanting it always to be there.

OF RESTAURANTS AND WHALING SHIPS

"But Stubb, he eats the whale by its own light, does he?
and that is adding insult to injury, is it?"
—MOBY DICK

On my life, I swear to you that duck fat will burn as bright as the oil of the leviathan and cleaner than any beeswax. There are boundless lessons to be learned from the modern-day Queequegs who inhabit the subcultural world that exists behind kitchen doors, especially in the finest restaurants. Like whaling ships, kitchens act as magnets to those who, like the biblical Ishmael, are banished from society by the very nature of their character. It is here that the oddest of characters will find freedom of personal expression and are ultimately molded into great artisans. Just as whalers gained reverence for the blubber they harvested and the versatile oil that it yielded, you will find among the staff of certain kitchens a corresponding reverence for duck fat. The greatest chefs know that the beauty of many foods is enhanced when sautéed in duck fat, and they substitute it for butter or olive oil whenever possible.

This appreciation, however, is not limited to culinary matters. Used to quiet the screeching hinges on old oven doors or as a soothing dressing for chapped lips, duck fat is an integral part of life in the kitchen. One maître d'/out-of-work actor, fretting over the lack of candles for his dining room, skeptically gave in to the prep chef with the grim reaper tatooed on her back, who suggested the substitution of duck fat. There was also the ex-patriate from Liverpool with six rings in one ear who landed in New York City washing dishes. His green leather-topped Doc Martin boots received a periodic coating of duck fat, which kept his feet warm and dry and protected the boots from ten hours of constantly dripping water. Finally, there was the poet/saucier who commuted home to Brooklyn late at night and who had been mugged on numerous occasions. Not wanting to carry a filet knife tucked in his sleeve, he decided on a more practical solution. After removing his dress whites and donning his street clothes, he would steal into the walk-in refrigerator, where the sacred fat was stored, and comb a spoonful of it into his hair.

After passing through the dining room with patrons still sipping coffee, he would bid good night to the floor staff, who had begun to notice his well-coiffed do. Once outside, he would quickly turn his jacket inside out and mess up his hair, smearing duck fat all over his face. Then he would descend into the subway, where he'd stare blankly at the walls and mutter his poetry under his breath.

To Render Fat

1 Trim all excess skin from the body of the duck, especially from around the neck and cavity. Pull out any fat from the interior of the cavity.

2 Cut it all up into small pieces and place in a heavy-bottomed saucepan with a tablespoon of water to prevent sticking.

3 Set the saucepan over low heat and gently cook the skin, stirring occasionally, for about two hours, or until it has become golden brown. Be careful not to cook it too fast, or the fat will brown or burn—the fat must stay clear. If your cracklings are not browning, strain them out and crisp them separately in a skillet with a little duck fat.

4 Strain the fat through a fine sieve and cool before refrigerating. The cracklings become crisper as they cool and taste better salted. If not using them right away, you will need to refrigerate them. If they are then to be used in a salad or as a garnish, reheat them briefly to take the chill off and serve at room temperature.

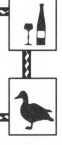

SAUCES

The dark, slightly gamy meat and crispy skin of the duck pair well with many flavors. All the sauces in this section are made from stock reductions with seasonings and tastes built in or incorporated near the end of cooking. Even without the skin, and although quite low in calories, duck meat can taste rich and therefore does not do well with cream- or butter-based sauces. What it needs is a sauce made from its own juices with the addition of complementary flavors.

In the classic tradition, duck is often paired with fruit sauces, although it is important to note that overly sweet, cloying fruit sauces are damaging to the delicate flavor of the duck. Adding fruit such as raspberries, cherries, or oranges to a reduction gives just the right degree of sweetness without the need for extra sugar. They also add the important element of acidity, which helps make every bite more delicious, instead of becoming dull and tiresome on the palate. Some of these sauces do have a small bit of butter swirled in at the end to give them a more silken texture and shine, and to add balance.

The cooking times and final quantity of all the sauces will depend on the quality of your stock. A thinner stock will have to be reduced longer and farther than a more gelatinous one to achieve the right taste and texture. Therefore, we have not included any cooking times in these recipes, although all quantities given are intended to produce enough sauce for at least two servings. You can estimate that the sauce will take about an hour to complete. If you are lucky enough to have ended up with more sauce than needed, you may freeze the rest.

If you are pressed for time, you can speed up the reduction by either boiling it very fast or making the sauce in a skillet. Making it in a skillet creates more surface area and therefore a faster reduction. Somehow, though, this does not produce as fine a sauce as does a slower method.

Sauces and Wine

The culinary cliché often derives from too rigid adherence to the classic traditions. Duck and Pinot Noir are a justifiably classic match. However, one can easily see that as an absolute rule it would be of little use within the context of this book, given the many methods of utilizing a duck. If there are any guidelines to adhere to in the wonderful anarchy of matching food and wine, they would include considering the garnish, that is, the sauce, over the main component of the dish and pairing it with a wine that is best equipped to address that influence. Developing a keen taste memory of both food and wine is, of course, an advantage when seeking out a wine that will interact well with a particular sauce. Most of us are able to summon our taste memory with very little effort as a source of nostalgic pleasure. Tasting wine stirs our memory to recall flavors that would seem to have nothing to do with wine or the flavors associated with grapes. A wine may be reminiscent of currants, citrus, or tropical fruit flavors, or of textures said to be buttery or chocolaty.

This sense memory, quite natural to most people, can be disciplined and developed in time to play an important role in the skill of food and wine matching. Before choosing a wine to accompany a particular dish, sample the sauce alone or with a piece of fresh bread. Take a moment of quiet concentration and summon up the flavors of a specific wine that might complement it. This is most effective as a process of elimination, to narrow down the number of considerations for accompaniment. Proper table manners for many of us include never gulping a beverage while food is still in your mouth, but begin the memory recall by imagining yourself indulging in this hedonistic habit. In some ways you will find this easier than having the wines there in front of you because in an instant you can conjure up one flavor, assess it, and move on to the next without the effects of palate fatigue or aftertaste.

Swallow the sauce and then contemplate how the surfaces inside your mouth have been affected by the coating of the various elements. Think about wine as a cleansing agent for a moment rather than a blending of flavors. The coating left in the mouth from a spicy sweet barbeque sauce will differ from that of a velvety beurre blanc or a sauce based on a heavily reduced duck stock. Acidity, alcohol, and sometimes oakiness will help cut through this coating.

Think of the body and weight of the sauce and the body and weight of the wine that is to follow it. In wine it is referred to as viscosity, the oily quality that gives a wine its "legs" on the side of the glass. A wine that is said to have a high viscosity, combined with a good acidity level, will serve as a good cleansing agent for a rich, full-bodied sauce.

Once the palate has been rinsed, there should be a blending of aftertastes of both the food and the wine, hopefully for a considerable length of time. As you have only the sauce at this time, consider the intensity of flavor it leaves and how subtle or powerful the wine flavors should be to counter or complement them. This is not a process that will result in earth-shattering combinations every time you attempt a food and wine match, but it does reduce the number of possibilities and bring one closer to turning the culinary experience into a memorable one.

Caramelized Honey Sauce

While this recipe calls for clover honey, a mild wildflower honey would also be delicious.

1   In a 1½-quart saucepan, heat the honey over medium-low heat. The honey will begin to bubble and brown. When it is caramelized but not burnt, about 1 to 2 minutes, take the pot off the stove.

2   Quickly add the wine. Be careful—the honey may splatter. Return the pot to a high flame and reduce the wine to ¼ cup.

3   Add the stock, bring to a boil, lower to a good simmer, and reduce the sauce until it is about ½ cup or until a saucelike consistency is achieved.

4   Season with the soy sauce, salt, and pepper.

There is almost no entrée that combines elegance with simplicity of preparation like the crispy-skinned breast of duck that has been sautéed rare and sliced into a fan cut. The positive first impression may quickly turn to skepticism when you present the unusual accompaniment of white wine with the duck breast. With the carmelized honey sauce, however, you may seduce your guests into amazement at how creatively the gamy strength of the duck can be harnessed by a variety of lush, exotic flavors. An abundance of rich tropical fruit in an almost fleshy-styled Chardonnay will stand up wonderfully to the rare meat once the honey sauce is added. The full-blown styles from California or Australia, with their complex flavors of tropical fruit, have an essential lushness that makes them preferable in this case to the more austere, crisp, or refined styles from France or Italy. For this combination of big fruit and sweetened gamy meat to be effective, a firm acidity in the wine is essential. Although there are many well-made Chardonnays in this style, a flabby acidity is the downfall of many. Duck is often associated with the colder months of the hunting season, yet this preparation will convince your guests that it is seasonally versatile. Light, fruity reds also work very well, but with white wine the dish takes on an unassuming air of complexity and elegant prettiness that is perfect for summertime dining.

Orange Sauce

MAKES AT LEAST
2 SERVINGS

Juice of 1 orange
¼ cup white wine
3 cups duck stock
1 (2-inch) strip orange zest
1 bay leaf
4 black peppercorns
Dash of Grand Marnier
Salt to taste

This differs from what most Americans think of as duck à l'orange. It is much less sweet and what sweetness is present is balanced by the slight bitterness of the orange rind. This is good with plain roasts and sautés, as well as duck with herb or cornmeal stuffing.

1   In a 1½-quart saucepan, bring the orange juice to a boil. Reduce it for 1–2 minutes, until it becomes syrupy but does not brown.

2   Add the wine and bring to a boil. Lower to a simmer and reduce by half.

3   Add the stock, zest, bay leaf, and peppercorns. Bring to a boil, lower to a good simmer, and reduce to ½ cup, or until a saucelike consistency is achieved.

4   Strain the sauce. Season with a dash of Grand Marnier and salt.

The sweet/tart combination blends well with the stronger gaminess of the duck meat, and this situation will allow you to take advantage of one of the most misunderstood and underrated wine values on the market—the powerful and exotic-flavored dry Alsatian or California Gewürztraminer. This orange sauce has a particularly intense, almost unctuous texture that seems to be too much for any other wine. In addition to a high level of acidity, Gewürztraminer has a weightiness that stands up to the sauce and, in fact, gives it a much lighter and classier feel. The richness of this orange sauce is an excellent complement to the stronger flavors of the meat, but this wine, with its spicy, floral elements, will bring on a heady experience reminiscent of orange blossoms.

Black Pepper Sauce

This elegantly spiced sauce is good paired with a plain roast or sauté, as well as a duck with an herb or apple stuffing.

1   In a 1½-quart saucepan, heat the oil over medium heat. Add the onion and garlic and brown, stirring occasionally.

2   Add the red wine, bring to a boil, lower to a simmer, and reduce to ¼ cup.

3   Add the stock, peppercorns, thyme, and bay leaf. Bring to a boil, lower to a good simmer, and reduce to ½ cup.

4   Strain the sauce and season with salt and the vinegar. When ready to serve, remove from the heat and swirl in the butter.

This is a very full-flavored, concentrated reduction sauce whose elegance of presentation can be deceptive when selecting a wine. Duck breast sliced into a fan cut has a classy appearance that might incline you to bring up the finest Burgundy or a well-aged Bordeaux. However, in this case you should think more country style—big rustic wines with forward fruit that don't have a lot of subtle nuances, which would ultimately be overpowered by the black pepper sauce. An interesting compromise might be found in some of the new-styled Tuscany reds from Italy, in which traditional grapes of the Chianti region are often blended with Cabernet or Merlot varietals. As is traditional in Bordeaux, these wines have the backbone derived from aging in small oak casks, but the concentration of fruit is less subtle or refined. Many red wines will work with the black pepper sauce; however, you will find that a wine with an almost overbearing lushness of fruit will be brought down to scale by the intensity of the sauce's flavors.

*MAKES AT LEAST
2 SERVINGS*

1 tablespoon vegetable oil
2 tablespoons chopped onion
1 clove garlic, chopped
½ cup red wine
3 cups duck stock
1½ teaspoons cracked black
peppercorns
Pinch of dry thyme
1 bay leaf
Salt to taste
¼ teaspoon red wine vinegar
¼ teaspoon unsalted butter

Madeira Sauce

MAKES AT LEAST
2 SERVINGS

1/3 cup red wine
3 cups duck stock
Pinch of dry thyme
4 peppercorns
2 teaspoons Madeira,
preferably Rainwater
Salt to taste
1/2 teaspoon unsalted butter

This is a richer, old-fashioned-tasting sauce, suitable for an elegant dinner. It is good paired with a plain roast or sauté, but also with the ballottine with spinach and pine nuts on page 100.

1   Bring the wine to a boil in a 1½-quart saucepan. Lower to a simmer and reduce by half.

2   Add the duck stock, thyme, and peppercorns. Bring to a boil, lower to a good simmer, and reduce to ½ cup, or until a saucelike consistency is achieved.

3   Strain the sauce and season with the Madeira and salt. When ready to serve, take the sauce off the heat and swirl in the butter.

The ingredients of the duck ballottine allow for white wine accompaniment, but when garnished with a Madeira sauce, it becomes a candidate for red wine. However, there are a few factors that warrant some precautionary thoughts. Starting with a rich gelatinous stock, adding a hearty red wine, seasonings, and Rainwater Madeira produces a very full-flavored, rich, old-fashioned-styled sauce. With gamier roasts of wild fowl, one might desire a heartier rustic-styled wine from Barolo or the Rhône region to really bear up to the sauce. But given that a commercially raised duck is likely to be used, the basis of the dish will be a meat of milder flavor and lighter texture. In this situation the sauce already has a very dominant influence over the meat, and adding a heavy, robust red wine is potentially overbearing. The combination of flavors is quite involved and the wine complement needs to be assertive, but through very subtle means. For instance, a Cabernet- or Merlot-based wine that is heavily barrel-fermented and bursting with ripe currantlike fruit may be categorized as an assertive wine, but one would hardly classify it as subtle. Grapes with a stronger flavor can make their impression without an overlushness of fruit or the backbone added by eighteen months in oak barrels. Varietals of such character include the Nebbiolo or the Sangiovese Grosso from Italy. These are, of course, the grapes of Barolo and Brunello, which will have a tendency to be too powerful for this situation. However, there are wines produced from these varietals that, although of lesser prestige on the market, will be a greater complement to the Madeira sauce. Lesser known varietals from Portugal are also characterized by strong flavors, though many of them will have very pronounced barrel flavors. Likewise for the Pinot Noir—unadorned, its varietal character can be very assertive, but find a producer that uses a minimal amount of barrel aging.

Raspberry Sauce

**MAKES AT LEAST
2 SERVINGS**

¾ cup white wine
3 cups duck stock
⅓ cup raspberries
2 teaspoons brandy
Salt and pepper to taste
½ teaspoon unsalted butter

This sauce is equally delicious made with blackberries. You can also use other fruits, such as cherries or plums. Be sure to use ripe berries, as unripe ones will make the sauce too tart. This goes especially well with a plain roast or sautéed breast.

1 In a 1½-quart saucepan, bring the white wine to a boil. Reduce it to ¼ cup.

2 Add the stock and bring to a boil. Lower it to a good simmer and reduce it for 15 minutes.

3 Add the raspberries. Continue reducing the sauce for another 15 minutes.

4 Pass the sauce through a sieve, pressing firmly on the solids. Return the strained sauce to the pot and finish reducing it to about ¾ cup, or until a saucelike consistency is achieved.

5 Season with the brandy, salt, and pepper. When ready to serve, take the sauce off the heat and swirl in the butter.

Any person who is a collector of fine wines knows the virtues of great patience. Yet only through the pains of wisdom and experiencing, after long anticipation, that a bottle has been aged for too long a time do we learn the danger of being over virtuous.

—HUGH GLOPPEN-JEROBOAM, SOMMELIER, DEW DUCK INN

With so many variables at work, the predictions of wine producers and writers do not always provide the means for cellaring wine to the state of perfection. Very often when a bottle has been held past its peak drinking time, the fruit begins to fade very quickly. This is not to say that the wine has actually begun to oxidize or that it will be ready for next week's salad, but merely that the beauty of its mature fruit has dried out and fallen from the remaining structure of the wine. The strategy is not foolproof but very often, depending on the stage of deterioration, a red wine in such a state can be very pleasantly revitalized by pairing it with a nice ripe raspberry sauce. Through this artificial means, the wine becomes quite palatable and may allow you to experience its remaining characteristics.

On the other hand, if you prefer a wine that is produced from excessively ripe fruit, the experience might turn gumdrop-like by the end of the entrée course. Actually, many types of red wine from many areas of the world will perform very well with the raspberry sauce, and like the White Wine Sauce on page 40, its flavors and texture will assist many wines that don't normally show very well with duck. Unlike the white wine sauce, however, the potently flavored raspberry sauce will bury the subtleties of your rare and finest properly aged wines.

White Wine Sauce

This is a simple sauce suitable for serving with a roast duck with sage and onion stuffing or something similar. To make an herb sauce, just add a tablespoon of chopped fresh herbs at the end. Sage, thyme, chives, parsley, and/or oregano are all complementary.

1　Heat the olive oil in a 1½-quart saucepan. Add the onion and sweat, stirring occasionally, for 5 minutes or until it is translucent.

2　Add the white wine, bring to a boil, and reduce by half.

3　Add the duck stock, bring to a boil, lower the flame, and reduce the sauce to about ½ cup or until a saucelike consistency is achieved. Season with salt and pepper.

This white wine sauce, while not fancy or formal enough for the elegant presentation of a sautéed duck breast, makes a wonderful moistening "gravy" for the carved meat of a roasted duck and its stuffing. Time and again, Pinot Noir has proven itself as the superior varietal with unadorned duck meat. The fruit of many other varietals seems to be deadened by the gaminess of even the mildest breeds of commercialized duck. As far as its relationship with wine is concerned, the beauty of the white wine sauce lies in its simplicity. Without being showy, it has the capacity to complement gaminess and at the same time mellow it out, allowing other wines to achieve much greater length of flavor on the palate. This sauce, served with simple roast duck, will offer smooth accompaniment for Cabernet or Merlot-based wines, youthful or well aged. You may experiment with a Rioja Reserva, a California Zinfandel, or many other reds from around the world that are not normally considered to be classic matches with duck.

Apple Cider Sauce

This sauce is wonderful with all varieties of duck and also with sautéed foie gras.

1   Heat the olive oil in a 1½-quart saucepan. Add the onion and sweat, stirring occasionally, for about 5 minutes or until it turns translucent.

2   Add the apple cider and wine. Bring to a boil and reduce to ¼ cup.

3   Add the stock and thyme and bring to a boil. Lower to a good simmer and reduce to about ½ cup or until a saucelike consistency is achieved.

4   Season with salt, pepper, and one of the brandies. When ready to serve, remove from the heat and swirl in the butter.

Of all the fruit sauces intended for duck, this is the one that is ultimately the least fruity in character. There is a pleasant element of tartness blended with the duck stock and herbs, but one would be hard-pressed to identify it as derived from fresh apple cider. The fact that this preparation has a very distinctive taste makes it conducive to many red wine varietals, and one need not recall the taste memory of apples. The classic Pinot Noir shows as well as ever, and a spicier California Zinfandel or the classier Rhône wines will also provide an interesting dimension.

MAKES AT LEAST
2 SERVINGS

1 tablespoon olive oil
1 small onion, peeled and diced
½ cup apple cider
¼ cup white wine
3 cups duck stock
Pinch of thyme
Salt and pepper to taste
Dash of either Calvados, applejack, or brandy
¼ teaspoon unsalted butter

Herb Vinaigrette

**MAKES
ABOUT ONE CUP**

1/3 cup white wine vinegar

2/3 cup good quality olive oil

1/4 cup chopped mixed fresh herbs (parsley, chives, tarragon, chervil, thyme)

Salt and pepper to taste

1 Place the vinegar in a bowl. Add the olive oil in a thin, steady stream, whisking constantly.

2 Add the herbs, salt, and pepper and combine thoroughly.

SOUPS AND SALADS

Wine with Soup

Many people consider wine with a soup course to be completely unnecessary, particularly if a clear soup is served as a starter. The preparation of such soups often includes the addition of a Madeira or sherry to add flavor and to sharpen the acidity of the soup. These same wines are pleasant sipping with those soups and add the contrasting sensation of something cold that some people may enjoy. Other wine choices might depend on the consistency of the soup. A chunky-style soup, served with fresh bread and intended to be a meal in itself, might call for a light, fruity wine to accompany it. In the classical repertoire there is the traditional crisp Provençal white wine served with a bouillabaisse or pistou. In most cases, however, it is the lack of variation in consistency, a sensation of wet on wet, rather than a clashing of flavors, that makes soup with wine problematic. Because of this, you may happen across flavor combinations that ought to blend very effectively but that prove to be mundane as a dining experience.

An interesting alternative is to turn a soup course into a two-sequenced taste adventure—first enjoying the soup and then experiencing the wine. The soup can be savored for all its richness, warmth, and depth of flavor without intermittent cooling sips of wine. After a hot soup

there lingers on the palate and olfactory senses a range of textural and flavor sensations. Consider these flavors for their power and length from the time the last spoonful of soup is tasted. The Duck Soup with Black Mushrooms and Ham (page 50) serves as an excellent example. The richly concentrated broth, flavored with the earthy mushrooms and lightly salty prosciutto, will leave the palate well primed. As the bowl is being lifted away, present your guests with a light but well-structured, fruity wine. These lingering flavors, while the mouth is still heated from the soup, will turn even a modest wine into a virtual burst of fruit and freshness. Any number of varietals will work very effectively. Consider, for instance, the Rieslings from the Rheinpfalz region in Germany. The delicate applelike fruit and floral character that many of them possess will shine forth in the surprisingly pleasant first few sips . . . a swooning segue into the cheese and salad course.

Potato Leek Soup with Confit

The confit in this soup is used more for its flavor than its meat. Simmered in the soup broth, the confit adds the perfume of its seasonings as well as an extra meatiness. Made a day ahead, not only will the flavors of this soup improve but the fat will harden for easy removal. Confit also pairs well with soups made from beans, cabbage, squash, and pumpkin.

1   Heat the olive oil in a 3-quart saucepan. Add the leeks and garlic and sweat over low heat for 10 minutes until softened.

2   Add the stock, bay leaf, thyme, and confit. Bring to a boil and simmer ½ hour.

3   Add the potatoes and simmer another ½ hour, until they are cooked through.

4   Season with salt and pepper.

Try any crisp and dry rosé or non-barrel-fermented white. Also see Wine with Soup, page 43.

SERVES 4

2 teaspoons olive oil

3 leeks, white part only, halved lengthwise and cut into ¼-inch slices

1 teaspoon finely chopped garlic

6 cups duck stock

1 bay leaf

1 teaspoon dry thyme

1 duck neck or wing confit

3 cups Idaho potato, peeled and cut into ½-inch dice

Kosher salt and pepper to taste

Consommé

SERVES 4

4 egg whites

½ cup minced vegetables
(carrot, celery, and onion,
including some skin)

1 plum tomato, minced

¼ pound ground beef

2 quarts duck stock, very cold

Kosher salt and pepper
to taste

Dash of port, sherry, or
Madeira (optional)

Consommé is a clarified stock. It can be very elegant and also very satisfying, particularly as a panacea on a winter day when you have a cold. When making consommé, it is especially important that you start with a good stock. There are many, slightly varying techniques for making it and sometimes, no matter how many times you have succeeded in the past, one day it just won't clarify. In this recipe I have added ground beef because it seems to make the process more foolproof. A dash of wine vinegar helps, too. There are endless ways to garnish consommé, using julienned vegetables, diced foie gras terrine, diced duck gizzard confit, diced duck tongues, slivers of duck meat, duck liver quenelles, poached "white kidneys" thinly sliced, and even nonduck foods. You can also infuse flavors such as ginger or mushrooms into the broth.

1   Place the egg whites in a mixing bowl and whisk them until frothy.

2   Add the vegetables, tomato, and ground beef to the egg whites and mix very thoroughly.

3   Add the chilled duck stock to the mixture and mix very thoroughly.

4   Pour everything into a 3½-quart saucepan and place over medium-low heat. Stir slowly and continually until the consommé just begins to boil. This might take up to half an hour. (Alternatively, you can place the consommé over very low heat and let it come to a boil without stirring. This will usually work, but you do take some risk that there will be some sticking and burning on the bottom.) Immediately lower the heat to a gentle simmer so that the consommé is moving. The solids and egg

whites should rise to the top and congeal in a good raft. If it is simmering too hard, the raft will break up.

5 Simmer for 45 minutes and turn off. Gently strain the consommé through several layers of cheesecloth, being careful not to break up the raft and leaving it behind in the pot. You will probably want to reduce the liquid somewhat to make a consommé of good strength. Just place the strained liquid in a clean pot and boil gently until it is the desired strength. Season with the salt, pepper, and one of the alcohols if desired.

A rich, deeply concentrated duck consommé is so soothing and satisfying that we're really going out on a pedantic limb by trying to better the experience with an accompanying beverage. But here are some observations. Consommé with a crisp dry fino sherry is fine. The fino is nonintrusive and somewhat refreshing; however, moving into other sherry categories is not a good idea. An Amontillado, for instance, turns bland and doesn't aid the course very much. A Sercial Madeira has a light sweetness and a very interesting effect on the consommé flavors, but again, other versions such as the sweeter Rainwater don't offer the sharpness needed to cut through the viscosity of the consommé. Most interesting, though, is the authentic dry Marsala, which has an amazing capacity to increase the flavor intensity of the consommé with intermittent sips.

Duck Minestrone

SERVES 6

1 cup diced onion

2 cloves garlic, finely chopped

2 tablespoons olive oil

1/4 cup white wine

6 cups duck stock

1 bay leaf

1 teaspoon dry oregano

1/3 cup diced carrot

2 cups diced zucchini

1/2 cup diced leek

2 cups diced mushrooms

2 branches fresh thyme

1/2 cup diced green beans

1 cup shredded savoy cabbage

1 1/2 cups diced, cooked duck meat

Kosher salt and pepper to taste

Freshly grated Parmesan cheese

This hearty soup is a good way to use cooked leftover duck meat. It can be served as an appetizer or paired with a green salad and some good bread for a complete meal. If you dice the vegetables that are to be added toward the end of the recipe while the ones you added earlier are simmering, the whole preparation will take no more than an hour.

1 In a noncorrosive 3½-quart saucepan, slowly sweat the onion and garlic in the olive oil for 5 minutes until soft.

2 Add the white wine, bring to a boil, and reduce by half.

3 Add the stock, bay leaf, and oregano. Bring to a boil, lower the heat to medium, and let the stock reduce for 15 minutes.

4 Add the carrots and simmer 1 minute.

5 Add the zucchini, leek, mushrooms, and thyme, and simmer until tender, about 10 minutes.

6 Add the green beans, cabbage, and duck meat. Simmer another 5 minutes.

7 Remove the thyme branches and bay leaf. Season to taste with salt and pepper.

8 Ladle into bowls. Pass the Parmesan and let your guests help themselves.

If you are using the minestrone as a single-course meal, it is hearty enough to warrant an accompanying wine. It is somewhat ironic, though,, that the less robust wines seem to make a nicer accompaniment. Given the quantity of vegetables in this soup, you are not likely to find any one perfect match, but fresh, clean, and dry wines such as a Pinot Blanc from Alsace or a variety of crisp Italian whites, such as Vernaccia, would be quite refreshing.

Duck Soup with Black Mushrooms and Ham

SERVES 2–4

3 cups duck stock

4 slices fresh ginger

2 scallions

6 dried shiitake mushrooms, soaked in water for 2 hours, drained, and sliced

1 teaspoon soy sauce

1/2 cup shredded Chinese or Napa cabbage

3 water chestnuts, sliced

1/4 teaspoon kosher salt

1 tablespoon shredded duck ham (see page 168) or prosciutto

As presented here, this soup can be either a first or a middle course. With the addition of leftover duck meat or perhaps red-cooked duck meat (see page 80), it can be a meal in itself.

1   In a 3-quart saucepan, bring the stock, ginger, and one of the scallions, sliced, to a boil. Simmer for 20 minutes and strain. Return the strained broth to the pot.

2   Add the mushrooms and simmer another 10 minutes.

3   Add the soy sauce, cabbage, water chestnuts, and salt, and heat until the cabbage is wilted, about 3 minutes.

4   Pour the soup into bowls and garnish with the duck ham and the other scallion, thinly sliced on the diagonal.

The combination of the very earthy black mushrooms and an occasional taste of saltiness from the duck ham makes the already problematic soup and wine combination very difficult. Normally, lighter, fruity wines will work best with a soup course, but most will not stand up to these ingredients. The very crisp Italian whites, such as Vernaccia or Verdicchio, come the closest. See Wine with Soup, page 43.

Crackling Salad

Crunchy cracklings can take the place of croutons in a salad. Make a good assortment of greens, with radicchio, watercress, Bibb, arugula, and the like. If you can find a mesclun mix (assorted wild greens), even better. Dress the salad with any vinaigrette, toss, and sprinkle with the cracklings.

Duck Liver Timbale Salad

SERVES 4

¼ pound duck livers
1 shallot, peeled and sliced
2 eggs
¾ cup heavy cream
¼ teaspoon kosher salt
2 teaspoons port
1 teaspoon brandy
Butter for greasing
1 small bunch watercress
1 tablespoon red wine vinegar
2 tablespoons olive oil
Kosher salt and pepper to taste
2 tablespoons cracklings

These molded warm custards are visually pleasing and an easy way to utilize duck liver.

1   Preheat the oven to 350°. Clean the livers by removing any visible veins or fat. Cut each one in half.

2   Combine the livers with the shallot, eggs, heavy cream, kosher salt, port, and brandy in a food processor or blender. Process until completely smooth.

3   Butter four ½-cup ramekins well. Fill with the liver mixture.

4   Place the ramekins in a water bath and bake for approximately 20 minutes or until the timbales have set.

5   Toss the watercress with the vinegar and olive oil and season to taste with the salt and pepper. Arrange the greens around four plates.

6   Invert the timbales onto the center of the salad and garnish with cracklings.

These may be made up to two days ahead and reheated, covered with aluminum foil, in a 350° oven for approximately 10 minutes.

There is more than one reason for the development of the champagne brunch. Eggs are a notorious enemy to almost any wine. Only champagne seems to have the high acidity to really accommodate the flavor and texture of eggs, and usually at the risk of losing some of authentic champagne's delicate subtleties. The duck liver timbale is an attractive appetizer that, at first, one would be inclined to match very easily with a variety of wines. Most, however, will prove ineffective because of the eggs that are used as a binding agent. Though they are only a small element here, and hardly a flavoring agent, their minor role will be detrimental to wine. Champagne is friendly and safe, but save your $25 and venture forth with a $10 bottle of dry Marsala. The authentic Marsala from Sicily has a taste not unlike that of aged sherry and some of the caramel flavors of Madeira. Marsala is actually a blend of heated and fortified wines that range in dryness. The Marsala's depth of flavors and barrel-aged fruit will penetrate the shield of the custard and absolutely intensify the liver to a richer, suppler flavor. With the mellow finish provided by the liver, the Marsala is figuratively retasted with greater depth of flavor, and the palate will easily bounce back and forth between these wonderful sensations for the duration of the course. Its hint of sweetness is subtle enough that progressing to a drier wine with the next course will not pose any problem, though the intensity of the liver might call for an interim salad or consommé as a palate cleanser.

Warm Duck Liver and Prosciutto Salad

SERVES 2

2 duck livers
1 large shallot
2 tablespoons shredded prosciutto
2 cups mixed greens (radicchio, watercress, endive, arugula, etc.)
5 teaspoons olive oil
1 tablespoon red wine vinegar
Kosher salt and pepper to taste

1 Clean the duck livers by removing any connecting veins and fat. Cut each one in 4 pieces.

2 Peel the shallot, trim off the ends, and slice it lengthwise in half.

3 Place the prosciutto and greens in a metal bowl.

4 In an 8-inch skillet, heat one teaspoon of the olive oil until it just begins to smoke. Add the duck livers and shallot and sauté very rapidly, tossing, for about 10 seconds, until the livers are browned but not cooked through.

5 Turn off the flame. Add the vinegar and the remaining 4 teaspoons of olive oil, and the salt and pepper. Pour the contents of the pan over the greens and toss. If the greens do not wilt slightly, place the whole bowl over a low flame and toss them for a few seconds until they wilt a little. Serve at once.

The meat elements in this dish are too minor to have any real impact on the choice of wine, especially since there are also shallots, red wine vinegar, and a variety of greens to contend with. You are likely to have some difficulty finding anything to serve with this particular salad course. There are, however, an increasing number of very dry, very dark rosés from California that possess very rich fruit. For drinking by themselves, you may not prefer their style to the more austere versions from France, but they are far more effective in this context. Many of them will add a refreshing raspberry or strawberry fruit to the combination, which seems to fit just right.

Duck Salad Chinois

1 (5-pound) Pekin duck, quartered, with boneless breasts

1½ teaspoons fresh ginger, grated

1 teaspoon finely chopped garlic

¾ teaspoon ground coriander seed

4 tablespoons sherry vinegar

3 tablespoons plus 2 teaspoons olive oil

2 tablespoons plus 1 teaspoon sesame oil

1 teaspoon soy sauce

½ teaspoon kosher salt

Pepper to taste

3 scallions

1 bunch watercress

12 snow peas, julienned

2 cups shredded Napa cabbage

This salad makes an excellent first course or a light, refreshing summer lunch. You may improvise the recipe to utilize duck meat left over from a previous meal.

1   Roast the duck legs for 45 minutes to an hour in a 350° oven until done. Let cool.

2   Heat a 10-inch skillet with an ovenproof handle until very hot. Add the duck breasts, skin side down, to the dry pan and lower the heat to medium (please see page 21, How to Cook a Duck Breast). Brown the skin side, turn over, and cook to the desired doneness (medium is best). Pour off the fat and reserve it for another use.

3   Remove the duck breasts from the pan and let cool.

4   Combine the ginger, garlic, coriander, vinegar, olive oil, sesame oil, soy sauce, salt, and pepper for the dressing.

5   Remove and discard the skin from the duck legs and breasts. Slice the breasts crosswise, holding your knife at a 45-degree angle, into ¼-inch slices. Bone the legs, making sure you remove any remaining fat. Dice the leg meat.

6   Cut the scallions diagonally into thin slices.

7   In a bowl, combine the duck meat, scallions, and dressing. Mix thoroughly and let marinate at least one hour at room tem-

perature. You can prepare this recipe up to one day ahead to this point and store it in the refrigerator. Be sure to bring the salad to room temperature before serving.

8   Divide the watercress, snow peas, and cabbage among your plates, arranging the greens in an attractive circle. Place the duck salad in the center of each plate. Drizzle any extra dressing over the greens.

The most distinguishing characteristic of the chinois salad is the pairing of flavors in the sesame oil and the very dark, barrel-aged sherry vinegar. The somewhat exotic essence of the sesame and the rich, almost balsamic-like quality of the aged sherry vinegar combine to make a very complex flavoring for the duck meat. It is a blend of flavors that is too pronounced to benefit from trying to equal that intensity with a rich, fat-styled wine. Such a situation usually calls for a wine that works on a much simpler level. One way to achieve this is by choosing a particular element of the dish and trying to enhance just that single aspect by adding a new flavor element to complement it or to add complexity. The obvious choice is a chilled, light, and very crisp fino sherry, which would be refreshing on a spring or summer afternoon. The flavor of the fruit is subtle but distinct and clean, adding to the depth of the salad dressing flavors. The character of both sherry elements seems to complement the sesame taste better than any other wine combination and its acidity cuts through the sesame oil lingering on the palate, making the dish as a whole seem lighter. Like all sherries, a fino will have a slightly higher alcohol content than wines that have not been fortified. The alcohol level adds to the crispness of the sherry, but one should be cautious of serving it as if it were a wine that is more easily quaffed, particularly in hotter climates. The classic, small capita, the traditional glass of the Jerez region in Spain, will encourage slower sipping.

Warm Duck Confit Salad with a Poached Egg

SERVES 2

4 cups mixed salad greens (watercress, arugula, chicory, radicchio, romaine)

2 radishes, cut in half and thinly sliced

1 tablespoon plus 1 teaspoon duck fat

½ loaf Italian bread, crust removed, cut into ½-inch cubes

Kosher salt and pepper to taste

1 large duck confit leg or 2 smaller legs or breasts

2 duck confit hearts and/or gizzards, sliced

2 eggs, preferably duck

Dash of vinegar

2 large shallots, cut in half and sliced lengthwise

3 tablespoons olive oil

2 tablespoons red wine vinegar

This makes a great brunch dish or summer lunch. You can start with whole pieces of confit, but it is also an excellent way to use up broken pieces.

1   Place the salad greens and radishes in a large metal mixing bowl.

2   Melt 1 tablespoon of the duck fat in a 10-inch skillet over medium heat. When hot, add the bread cubes. Cook the croutons, tossing occasionally, until they are golden but still soft inside. Sprinkle with salt and add to the salad.

3   Remove and discard the skin from the confit legs and/or breasts. Break the meat into rough, bite-size pieces.

4   Melt the remaining 1 teaspoon duck fat in the skillet over high heat. Add all the confit and quickly sauté until it is browned and crisped. While the duck is browning, poach the eggs in simmering water with a dash of vinegar added.

5   Add the shallots to the duck and cook another 30 seconds.

6   Turn off the flame. Add the olive oil and vinegar. Heat through, stirring, and pour over the salad.

7   Season the salad with salt and pepper. Toss. If the greens have not slightly wilted from the hot dressing, place the whole bowl over a low flame and toss the salad until it wilts a little.

8   Divide the salad between two plates and top each one with a poached egg.

Fortunately, sparkling wine is very popular at brunch and there will be no need to change any habits. Any nice, light, unassuming sparkling wine with pleasant fruit and good acidity will provide a cheerful accompaniment for this salad. At lunch a Sauvignon Blanc in a light, fruity style will be well suited. Do not, however, attempt to serve one of the grassy or herbacious-style Sauvignon Blancs, which will prove to be too aggressive and harsh for such simple fare.

APPETIZERS

Canapés and Wine

Organizing a variety of canapés can prove very interesting, particularly when exploring the wines usually associated with before-dinner aperitifs. Too often the predinner situation is randomly addressed with a dry white wine, a celebratory champagne, or worse, by leaving the flavors of the canapés open to assault by the guests' preference from an open bar. If the labor is invested to provide a selection of canapés, it is worth taking full control of your guests' palates right from the beginning. This may entice you into sampling the broad range of affordable and interesting aperitifs that are too often left unconsidered by most consumers. Madeira is available in a range from pale and dry Sercial to a portlike sweet Malmsey. Sherry has an even greater range, with major sherry houses having as many as eighteen different styles to choose from. From Cognac there is the Pineau des Charentes, which is lightly sweet and largely undiscovered by the American consumer. None of the canapés in this chapter conflict with a full-bodied champagne, but neither do they provide the type of marriage that would really command your attention. The suggestions following these recipes offer a few combinations that come closer to that type of match.

Duck Liver Mousse

MAKES
APPROXIMATELY
4-DOZEN 1-INCH CANAPÉS

1-pound duck livers
3 tablespoons unsalted butter
1 medium shallot, chopped
1 1/2 teaspoons chopped garlic
2 tablespoons brandy
3/4 teaspoon kosher salt
1/4 teaspoon ground
black pepper
1 tablespoon Madeira,
preferably Rainwater

This spreadable pâté is delicious as an hors d'oeuvre. It may be set out in a bowl for guests to help themselves or piped onto toasts. It may also be formed with two spoons into an egg shape, garnished with cracklings, and served with garlic toast as an appetizer. The raw livers may be saved each time you cook a duck and frozen until there are enough of them to make a mousse.

1   Clean the livers by removing any connecting veins and visible fat. Cut them in half.

2   In a 10-inch skillet, melt the butter over low heat. Add the shallot and garlic. Cook slowly, stirring occasionally, for 5 minutes, until they are soft.

3   Add the livers and cook over medium heat, stirring occasionally, for about 2 minutes.

4   Take the skillet off the stove, add the brandy, and return it to the fire. *Be careful*—the brandy will ignite. Continue cooking for another 2 minutes, leaving the livers still rosy inside.

5   Pour everything from the skillet into the bowl of a food processor. Process until smooth, about 1 minute. For a finer texture, you can pass the mousse through a sieve.

6 Scrape the mousse into a bowl and season with the salt, pepper, and Madeira. Cover with plastic wrap and chill until firm but still spreadable. This will keep for about a week in the refrigerator.

This mousse is obviously stonger and earthier in flavor than the mousse of foie gras (page 64). Even the texture is less smooth, partly because of the natural state of the liver and because this mousse is bound without cream. Here the middle-range Madeiras —Rainwater and Verdelho—provide the nicest balance. Their sweetness becomes almost imperceptible and the flavors of earth and wood, along with the dark, aged character of the fruit, blend with considerable length, as the combination lingers on the palate. An odd contrast is found with the Pineau des Charentes. Its fresh fruit loses all its body and charm and in this context comes across cloyingly sweet. Served this canapé, your guests will be provided with a marvelous burst of flavor, but possibly one that is too intense to really blend well with any of the white wines that are traditionally used as aperitifs. Most will be overpowered rather than overtly offend anyone's palate. Fuller-bodied sparkling wines will have an advantage over most still wines.

Foie Gras Mousse

This mousse may be served on its own, piped onto toast for an attractive canapé, or incorporated into a terrine (see page 91).

1   Clean the foie gras according to the directions on page 26.

2   Marinate the foie gras overnight in the brandy, Sauternes, or port; white wine; and kosher salt.

3   Remove the foie gras from the liquid and bring the marinade to a boil. If there is not enough liquid to cover the foie gras, add water. Reduce the marinade to a simmer and add the foie gras.

4   Poach at a very low simmer for about 15 minutes, or until a skewer inserted into the liver comes out warm.

5   Remove the foie gras from the liquid and chill.

6   Cut the foie gras into 1-inch pieces and place in a food processor. Process 10 seconds. Add the cream all at once and process another 20 seconds.

7   Slowly add the melted butter, watching to be sure it is incorporated. Stop adding butter if the mousse looks like it is not absorbing anymore and might curdle. Process until smooth. Do not overprocess or it will curdle.

8   Scrape the contents of the processor into a bowl. Season with the salt, pepper, and port. Chill until firm but still spreadable.

MAKES APPROXIMATELY 2-DOZEN 1-INCH CANAPÉS

8 ounces foie gras, grade B

½ cup brandy

½ cup Sauternes or port

½ cup white wine

2 teaspoons kosher salt

½ cup heavy cream

4 tablespoons melted butter, cooled to room temperature

Salt and white pepper to taste

2 teaspoons port

With such a smooth, delicate texture, the foie gras mousse, when served as a canapé, should not be subjected to random sloshing, but should be washed down with the greatest reverence. A Sercial, the lightest-style Madeira, has a very delicate flavor that really parallels the mousse very elegantly. However, the mousse is quickly overpowered by the darker and sweeter-style Madeiras. The drier versions of Marsala are also a very pleasing accompaniment. Those who dream of foie gras with Sauternes but are averse to the notion of such richness as a precursor to a full meal should experience the Pineau des Charentes. This refreshing aperitif will serve as a dazzling micro version of the more classic combination.

The foie gras mousse has a wider range of white wine potential than slices of sautéed foie gras. The addition of butter and cream mellows the taste as well as affecting the texture. With this preparation, the fruit of full-bodied Chardonnays or sparkling wines with a good acidity are more likely to shine through. Although acidity is still crucial, sweeter wines should not be overlooked. Riesling and Chenin Blanc are both worth considering.

White Kidneys *

These are a surprisingly pleasant addition to the lightly and politely serving-up of the inner organs of beasts and fowl. Mr. Leopold Bloom would likely find them much more mildly flavored and delicately textured than his usual morning fare. They are, in fact, quite white and astonishingly large, and their rich and smooth consistency hints of a livery earthiness that makes them very conducive to the adornment of a wide range of sauces, such as a remoulade or mustard sauce. Poached or rapidly sautéed, they can be used as a canapé or as garnish for another dish. Their taste is mellow enough that champagne or any of your finest whites will help turn them into a rather luxurious appetizer.

---

* *White kidneys* is a euphemism for testicles.

Duck Rillettes

MAKES
ABOUT 2½ CUPS

3 cups rendered duck fat (or
substitute lard)
1 five-pound Pekin duck,
quartered, with
boneless breasts
1 tablespoon finely
chopped garlic
1 tablespoon finely
chopped shallot
1½ teaspoons ground
black pepper
2 teaspoons kosher salt
½ teaspoon ground allspice
¼ teaspoon ground nutmeg
2 teaspoons dry thyme

Rillettes are hearty, rustic, stick-to-the-ribs food, which are usually made from duck, goose, or pork. It is a peasant dish of French origin made by simmering meat very slowly in fat, then pulling it into shreds. The shredded meat is seasoned, combined with some of the fat, and packed into a crock. Spreading rillettes onto freshly baked bread while enjoying a chilled Beaujolais, especially out of doors, is one of life's ultimate gustatory pleasures.

While time-consuming to prepare, rillettes keep indefinitely. You can expedite the preparation by using a food processor to chop the meat, but the technique of pulling the meat apart into fine shreds with two forks produces rillettes of superior texture that are their own reward.

The average quiche becomes the famous Quiche de Touraine simply by adding a layer of rillettes. To serve the rillettes as an hors d'oeuvre, spread them on toasts or set them out in an attractive crock for guests to help themselves. As an appetizer, serve them in individual ramekins or simply as a hearty spoonful garnished with some greens. Be sure to have plenty of toasts or a fresh baguette.

1 Melt the fat in a 3-quart saucepan. Add the duck and simmer very slowly until it is very tender and falling off the bone, about three hours.

2 Remove the duck from the fat. When it is cool enough to handle, remove and discard all skin and bones. Break the duck up into chunks.

3 With the back of a fork, mash the duck to break it up more. Then, with two forks held upside down and pulling in opposite directions, shred the meat. When finished, you should have a pile of fine, even fibers. This takes patience, but it is worth it.

4 In a 10-inch skillet, place 6 tablespoons of duck fat and the shredded duck. Add all the seasonings and stir to mix thoroughly.

5 Over low heat, gently heat the rillettes for 5 minutes, until the seasonings have blended with the meat and are no longer raw. Be careful not to brown the rillettes.

6 Pack the rillettes, not too tightly, into a porcelain or stone-ware casserole or crock. Pour over ½ cup melted, but not hot, duck fat—just enough to saturate the meat. Refrigerate.

　　　To preserve the rillettes, let them set in the refrigerator until firm. Add another ½-inch layer of melted, not hot, duck fat and refrigerate again until firm. Then wrap in foil. When serving rillettes, temperature is important. It should be warm enough to release the flavors but cool enough to maintain their smooth consistency.

Rillettes are yet another duck preparation that simply by the nature of their versatility are valuable to have in the house at all times. Once the endeavor has begun, you will realize that the ritual of production is rather entertaining, and if you make a big batch, it will keep for a considerable length of time. You can enjoy a hearty open-faced sandwich, kicking back with your favorite quaffing red wine or beer. Or on the finer side, they can be served as a canapé on toast points at even the most elegant gatherings. Among the aperitifs that might be matched with rillettes are the Pineau des Charentes; the blend of sweet wine and salty spread is particularly effective. The Sercial Madeira combines with the spices to create flavors hinting at lavender, that are most surprising and pleasing. As an appetizer, rillettes can be matched with very fine white wines, particularly those that contain a slight amount of sweetness, such as Chenin Blanc or Riesling.

Canapé of Duck Heart and Gizzard Confit with Roquefort Butter

MAKES 1 DOZEN

5 teaspoons unsalted, softened butter

7 teaspoons Roquefort cheese, at room temperature

Pepper to taste

Dash of port

1 tablespoon chopped walnuts (optional)

6 assorted duck heart and gizzard confits, at room temperature

12 toasts, made from a baguette

Chopped parsley for garnish

1   Combine thoroughly in a bowl the butter, Roquefort, pepper, port, and walnuts (if desired).

2   Cut the heart and gizzard confit into thin slices.

3   Spread a teaspoon of the Roquefort butter on each toast and arrange the confit on top. Garnish with the chopped parsley.

Roquefort cheese has a sharp, piquant, and creamy saltiness that finishes with wet stone or earthy impressions. Adding butter and the spice of confit makes for a very complex and exciting flavor combination that will be enhanced by a wine with fruit and a touch of sweetness. The fruit of a Pineau des Charentes is quite fresh, being less altered by barrel treatment than most sherries or Madeiras, and its light sweetness makes this broad range of flavors come together quite harmoniously. The Sercial and Verdelho Madeiras, whose fruit has a slightly burnt, honeylike caramel taste made tolerable by a sharp acidity, also work well and on a very different level. The aged character of the fruit of these wines gives smoky overtones to the canapé. One or two samples of this perfect palate teaser create a sense of anticipation that tells your guests something special is going to follow.

To enhance the special occasion when a vintage port is uncorked, accompany it with the Roquefort canapé. These wonderful flavors enjoyed by a fireplace on a winter evening, will provide an infinitely memorable sense of warmth.

Duck Pâté

For summertime gatherings, pâté on fresh bread is a wonderful staple that can be prepared in advance and is practical for serving large numbers. It keeps well and can be served as a canapé or a well-regarded appetizer, even on formal occasions. There is, however, something special about eating pâté out of doors at a leisurely, shady picnic that is likely to precede a nice, lazy nap. Pâté is also seasonally versatile. Served up in heartier portions during fall or winter gatherings, it is an insulating sustenance food. Both of the recipes that follow have a peppery, garlicky spiciness that can be complemented by a variety of zesty mustards. Cornichons or other pickled vegetables garnish the plate with additional colors and provide a refreshing acidity, as well as adding complexity to the rustic earthiness of the pâté.

In the United States, pâté seems to have a bit of mystique, but you need not be intimidated, because pâté is actually quite easy to make, and we hope these versions will inspire you. A meat grinder is essential, but lacking one, grinding is a service that any good butcher should gladly provide. Try varying these recipes to create your own signature duck pâté to have on hand year round and to offer as gifts during the holidays.

Duck Pâté, Country Style

2 pounds uncooked duck meat

1 pound pork fat back plus approximately ¾ pound thinly sliced fat back or bacon

1 cup red wine

⅓ cup brandy

4 bay leaves

2 teaspoons dry thyme

5 cloves garlic, peeled and crushed

1 small onion, peeled and sliced

3 ounces bacon

4 duck livers

1 tablespoon kosher salt

1½ teaspoons ground black pepper

½ teaspoon ground white pepper

¼ teaspoon ground clove

¼ teaspoon ground nutmeg

½ teaspoon dry sage

¼ teaspoon ground allspice

1   Cut the duck meat and the one pound of fat back into pieces that will fit through your meat grinder. (A food processor is not a substitute.) In a bowl, combine them with the wine, brandy, bay leaves, 1 teaspoon of the thyme, and the garlic and onion. Cover and marinate overnight in the refrigerator.

2   Remove and discard the bay leaves. Drain and discard the liquid. Pass the solids, plus the bacon and livers, through a meat grinder fitted with the coarse-grinding plate, twice.

3   Add all the seasonings, the egg, the flour, and the browned onion. Mix very thoroughly.

4   Line a 5-cup terrine with the sliced fat back or bacon, leaving enough overhanging the edge to cover the top of the pâté. Fill with the pâté mixture, packing it in well, and cover with the fat.

5   Wrap the whole terrine in aluminum foil and place in a water bath.

6   Bake in a 350° oven for 1 hour and 15 minutes, or until the pâté is surrounded by a thin border of melted fat and a skewer inserted in the center comes out warm/hot.

7   Remove the terrine from the water bath and drain the water. Place the terrine back in the empty bath or on a sheet pan. Cover it with another sheet pan and weight it with about 10 pounds.

8   When the pâté has cooled completely, remove the weight. Wrap in plastic and refrigerate at least one day before serving.

9   To unmold, unwrap the pâté and place it on a sheet pan in a warm oven until the surrounding fat has melted and the pâté can be inverted. Never serve pâtés directly from the refrigerator, but they are best eaten slightly cool.

This country-style pâté is particularly well suited for summertime and picnic settings. It has an easy seasoning that lends itself favorably to a variety of white wines. Full and fruity-styled Chardonnays from California and Australia work, as well as crisp and dry whites such as those from the Rioja or Rueda regions in Spain. A clean and dry Provençal rosé would bring color to the combination.

The fully garnished pâté, with mustards and pickled vegetables, requires a wine with power and acidity, but a light sweetness could also play an important role. More powerfully flavored wines might include the Rieslings of the Rheingau region in Germany, the dry Alsatian Gewürztraminer, or its often sweeter American counterpart. The Chenin Blanc from Vouvray or California is a bit subtler but offers hints of sweetness with a real sense of freshness. The more affordable versions of these wines should work well in picnic situations, with the classier versions reserved for the more structured sit-down dinner where pâté is served as a first course or as a small canapé on toast.

Red wines also create a wonderful balance with this meat. The intense raspberry fruitiness and high acidity that a Beaujolais Villages achieves in a good vintage blends well with the peppery meat and cuts through the slight fattiness that provides for a smoother texture. A variety of medium or fuller-bodied reds, such as Rioja Crianza or Valdepeñas from Spain, Dolcetto d'Alba from Italy, or California Zinfandel, will also work. When choosing bigger reds or whites, there will be a point where a pronounced oakiness becomes astringent in this situation.

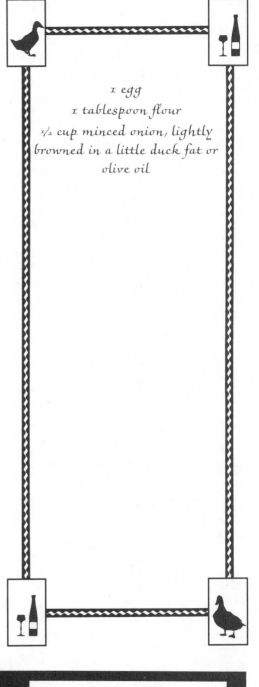

1 egg
1 tablespoon flour
½ cup minced onion, lightly browned in a little duck fat or olive oil

Duck Pâté with Confit

MAKES 1 PÂTÉ, APPROXIMATELY 20 SERVINGS

2 pounds uncooked duck meat

1 pound pork fat back plus approximately ¾ pound thinly sliced pork fat back or bacon

1 cup red wine

½ cup brandy

5 bay leaves

4½ teaspoons dry thyme

6 cloves garlic, peeled and crushed

1 small onion, peeled and sliced

5 ounces duck leg or breast confit

3 duck livers

1 tablespoon kosher salt

1½ teaspoons ground black pepper

½ teaspoon ground white pepper

1   Cut the duck meat and the one pound of fat back into pieces that will fit through your meat grinder. In a bowl, combine them with the wine, brandy, bay leaves, 2 teaspoons of the thyme, the garlic, and the onion. Cover and marinate overnight in the refrigerator.

2   Remove and discard the bay leaves. Drain and discard the liquid. Pass the solids plus the 5 ounces of leg or breast confit and the livers through a meat grinder fitted with a coarse-grinding plate, twice. Pass half of the mixture through a third time.

3   Add all the seasonings, the egg, the flour, and the browned onion. Mix very thoroughly.

4   Line a 5-cup terrine with the sliced fat back or bacon, leaving enough overhanging the edges to cover the top of the pâté.

5   Fill the terrine one-quarter full with the pâté mixture. Place a row of heart and gizzard confit down the center. Add another layer of pâté mixture to fill the terrine halfway, then another row of confit. Fill the terrine with the rest of the mixture. Rap the terrine on the counter to pack it in well. Cover with the overlapping fat or bacon.

6   Wrap the whole terrine in aluminum foil and place in a water bath.

7   Bake in a 350° oven for 1 hour and 15 minutes, or until the pâté is surrounded by a thin border of melted fat and a skewer inserted into the center comes out warm/hot.

8   Remove the terrine from the water bath and drain the water. Place the terrine back in the empty bath or on a sheet pan. Cover it with another sheet pan and weight it with about 10 pounds.

9   When the pâté has cooled completely, remove the weight. Wrap in plastic and refrigerate at least one day before serving.

10   To unmold, unwrap the pâté and place it on a sheet pan in a warm oven until the surrounding fat has melted and the pâté can be inverted. Never serve pâtés directly from the refrigerator, but they are best eaten slightly cool.

The confit and additional garlic and spice make for a hearty pâté not suited to serving with dry white wine although those with some sweetness will show through better. Lighter reds will do, but don't hesitate to go for the fuller-bodied rustic reds, such as those of the Rhône region, which are so pleasing during the colder months. See commentary following country-style pâté (page 71).

¼ teaspoon ground clove
¼ teaspoon ground nutmeg
¼ teaspoon ground allspice
Dash of cayenne
1 egg
1 tablespoon flour
½ cup minced onion, lightly browned in a little duck fat or olive oil
12 pieces duck heart and/or gizzard confit

Sautéed Duck Livers with Mushrooms

SERVES 2

2 teaspoons olive oil

4 ounces mushrooms, preferably cremini or fresh shiitake

1 small shallot, minced

3 duck livers, cleaned and deveined, cut into three pieces each

1/3 cup duck demi-glace

1 teaspoon heavy cream

Dash of port

Squeeze of lemon

Salt and pepper to taste

1 teaspoon chives, cut into 1/4-inch pieces

1   Heat the olive oil in an 8-inch skillet until very hot. Add the mushrooms and brown over high heat 1 minute.

2   Add the shallot and continue cooking over moderately high heat for 2–3 minutes, or until the mushrooms are nicely browned. Add more oil if the pan becomes dry.

3   Raise the heat to high and add the livers. Sauté, stirring occasionally, for about 30 seconds, until the livers are rosy inside. Remove the livers to two warmed plates.

4   Add the demi-glace and cream to the pan and reduce for about 1 minute, to a light saucelike consistency.

5   Season with the port, lemon, salt, pepper, and chives. Pour over the duck livers and serve.

Liver and Chianti is a northern Italian favorite; however, the combination falls short in both these situations. Liver and mushrooms provide a strong earthy component and the shallot and mustard a sweet zesty quality. In the first combination, the key is to slip in a light fruity element without further complicating the existing flavors. It is the cream in both these dishes that acts as an important determinant.

With the mushrooms and shallot, the cream is very light, but still enough in evidence to deter a match with a nice red wine. Dry crisp whites seem to work most efficiently, and although lighter whites are easily overpowered by the other very pronounced flavor elements, nice full Chardonnays work very well. Be wary of barrel aging—the strong earthiness of the liver and mushrooms is so prominent that any pronounced oakiness in a wine will clash with those elements. Chardonnays with minimal barrel fermentation or a generic Bourgogne Blanc will work very well.

For the shallot and mustard preparation, quite the opposite is true. In fact, the heavier cream content in this dish allows for a richer and oakier white wine. The cream serves to ease the oak and earthiness conflict, permitting the fruit to come through and blend with the shallot-sweetened liver and the subtle mustard flavor. Try your favorite full-bodied California or Australian Chardonnays.

Sautéed Duck Liver with Shallots and Mustard Cream

1 1/2 teaspoons olive oil
1 large shallot, peeled and thinly sliced lengthwise
3 duck livers, cleaned and deveined, cut into 3 pieces each
1 tablespoon duck demi-glace
1/3 cup heavy cream
1 teaspoon Dijon mustard
Salt and pepper to taste
Squeeze of lemon

1   Heat the olive oil in an 8-inch skillet. Add the shallot, and over moderate heat, sauté about 2 minutes, until browned.

2   Raise the heat to high, add the livers, and sauté for about 30 seconds, until they are rosy inside.

3   Remove the livers from the pan to two warmed plates.

4   Add the demi-glace and cream to the pan. Cook 30 seconds.

5   Add the mustard and reduce the cream to a light saucelike consistency.

6   Season with the salt, pepper, and lemon. Pour over the livers and serve.

See wine commentary following Sautéed Duck Livers with Mushrooms (page 75).

Duck and Butternut Squash Ravioli with Brandy and Black Pepper

MAKES ONE DOZEN,
TO SERVE FOUR
AS AN APPETIZER
OR TWO
AS AN ENTRÉE

¾ cup cooked duck meat,
coarsely chopped

⅓ cup cooked butternut
squash puree

1 tablespoon cut chives

¾ teaspoon chopped fresh
thyme

½ teaspoon salt

½ teaspoon freshly ground
black pepper

¼ teaspoon finely chopped
garlic

Fresh pasta dough
(see page 79)

Flour for dusting

1 egg, beaten (for egg wash)

2 teaspoons olive oil

¼ cup brandy

1 tablespoon unsalted butter

Salt to taste

1   Combine the duck meat, squash, chives, thyme, salt, ¼ teaspoon of the black pepper, and the garlic, and mix thoroughly.

2   Roll the pasta dough into two thin sheets, according to the directions for your machine. Keep the pasta sheets on a floured board, covered with plastic wrap or a slightly damp cloth.

3   Lightly dust your ravioli mold with flour. Lay one pasta sheet on top of it. With a pastry brush, lightly but thoroughly brush egg wash along the borders of each ravioli.

4   Fill each ravioli with the duck mixture. Place the second sheet of pasta dough on top and press gently with the palms of your hands to push out any air and seal lightly.

5   Using a rolling pin, seal and cut out the ravioli by rolling along the top of the mold. Turn the mold over to release the ravioli.

6 Cook the ravioli in 4 quarts of boiling, salted water for approximately 3 minutes, until al dente. Carefully drain. You may prepare this recipe one day ahead up to this point. If doing so, cool the ravioli with cold water, drain well, toss with a little olive oil, and refrigerate.

7 In a 10-inch noncorrosive skillet, heat 2 teaspoons olive oil. Add the ravioli to the skillet and sauté over medium heat until lightly browned, shaking the pan to toss them about 1 minute.

8 Remove the pan from the heat. Add the brandy, the butter, the remaining ¼ teaspoon pepper, and salt to taste. Raise the heat to high and return the pan to the heat. *Be careful*—stand back while you do this. The brandy will ignite. When the flame dies down, toss the ravioli and serve.

These fresh ravioli are a wonderful, economical way to use leftovers. Serve them as an appetizer or to accompany a salad for a light and healthy lunch. The squash has a creamy consistency and a slight sweetness that is highlighted by the chive and pepper. The duck meat will be somewhat inconspicuous, adding texture and working almost as a seasoning element for the ravioli.

Monterey or central coast California Chardonnay or Australian Chardonnay usually has the rich lushness of fruit to make a pleasant pairing. However, with the rather substantial consistency of the combined pasta and squash, a wine with a high viscosity is essential. You can try your favorite Chardonnay but it is in danger of appearing lighter in body next to this dish and will not really show through as you might think. The one varietal that has the power to stand up brilliantly is the dry Alsatian Gewürztraminer. These wines in better vintages have a nice weighty viscosity and rich scent that some might find reminiscent of duck fat, but it is their intense depth and spicy, exotic fruit that blend so wonderfully with the sweet, spicy squash and meat to elevate this dish to a whole new level of dining.

Basic Pasta Recipe

1   Place the flour in a mixing bowl and make a well in the center.

2   Combine the rest of the ingredients and pour them into the well.

3   Using a fork, stir the liquids in a circular motion, slowly incorporating the flour. Use your hands when the dough becomes too stiff.

4   Turn the dough out onto a floured board and knead until it becomes smooth and elastic, about 10 minutes. Cover in plastic and let rest, refrigerated, for at least one hour before using.

TO MAKE FETTUCCINE

1   Roll out the pasta according to the directions for your machine. Cut the sheets into 12-inch lengths and roll them up lengthwise.

2   Using a very sharp knife, cut the pasta at ½-inch intervals, in the same direction it has been rolled. Separate the strands immediately, toss them with a little flour, and strew them on a sheet pan. Cover with plastic and refrigerate.

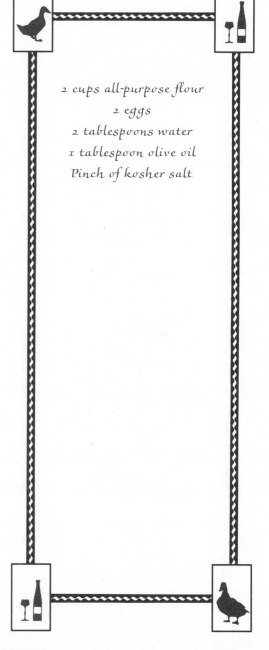

2 cups all-purpose flour
2 eggs
2 tablespoons water
1 tablespoon olive oil
Pinch of kosher salt

Bean Curd Roll with Red-Cooked Duck Tongues

SERVES 4

½ pound duck tongues

1 cup soy sauce

3 cups water

¾ cup sugar

1 teaspoon five-spice powder

¼ cup rice wine

4 ¼-inch slices ginger

2 cloves garlic, crushed

¼ pound fresh shiitake mushrooms

2 teaspoons plus ¼ cup soy oil

2 sheets dry bean curd skin

1 scallion, thinly sliced

R ed-cooking is a Chinese technique from the Fukien region in which a rich soy sauce–based, spiced broth is used to infuse flavor and color. It is most commonly used with poultry, fowl, and pork. Duck tongues, however, are by themselves quite bland and are most interesting for their unctuous and slightly crunchy texture. Red-cooking gives them an added dimension that transforms them into an unusual and delicious dish. Bean curd skin is the film that forms on top of cooking soybeans in the process of making bean curd and can be bought dried or fresh in Chinese markets. It has a nice, slightly chewy texture that makes a wonderful and nutritious wrapper. In the Chinese preparation of "mock duck," bean curd skin simulates the texture of duck skin.

1   Blanch the tongues in boiling water for ten minutes. When cool enough to handle, cut around the base of the tongue and pull out the bone. Remove the cartilage running down the underside of the tongue.

2   In a 2-quart saucepan, place the soy sauce, water, sugar, five-spice powder, rice wine, ginger, and garlic and bring to a boil.

3   Add the tongues to the liquid and lightly simmer ½ hour. Remove from the heat and let the tongues cool in the liquid.

4 Slice the mushrooms into ½-inch pieces. In a 10-inch skillet, heat the 2 teaspoons soy oil over high heat and rapidly sauté the mushrooms until browned, about 3 minutes.

5 Dip the bean curd sheets in boiling water until soft enough to work with, about 30 seconds. Lay them out flat on a work surface and pat dry.

6 Drain the duck tongues and reserve the liquid. (The red-cooking liquid may be stored in the refrigerator and used over and over indefinitely. Cooking a variety of meats in it will add to its depth and complexity.)

7 Divide the tongues and mushrooms between the two bean curd sheets, placing them along the edge closest to you and leaving at least 1 inch at each end. Fold in the sides and roll up the skins.

8 In a 10-inch skillet, heat the ¼ cup soy oil until it begins to smoke. Add the bean curd rolls, flap side down, to the oil. Quickly brown them on all sides. Remove to a dinner plate.

9 Moisten the rolls with ½ cup of the red-cooking liquid. Place the plate in a steamer and steam over water until the rolls are soft, 30–40 minutes. Remove to a cutting board.

10 Slice the rolls diagonally and divide among 4 plates. Pour the red-cooking liquid they were steamed with over them, garnish with the scallion, and serve.

Several of the ingredients in red-cooking—soy sauce, five-spice powder, ginger, and sugar—are likely to have a very overpowering effect on most wines. Sweetness in wine will be an asset, but look for something refreshing rather than heavy. Vouvray works very well, as will other lightly sweet wines often mixed with Chinese dishes. There are, however, wines made from a variety of other fruits such as apple or pear that are currently available from reputable producers here in the United States and that will provide an unusual accompaniment to this interesting dish. In their early youth, up to about eighteen months, these wines have an almost unparalleled freshness of fruit. They are simple and clean and will rinse the palate very effectively so that a dimension of fruit is added to the red-cooked flavor.

Wine with Foie Gras

Most methods of preparing sautéed foie gras include somewhat aggressive sauces, usually with high levels of acidity. These sauces might contain vinegar, onions, or sweet and sour flavorings, all of which add a sharpness that cuts through the rich, creamy texture of the foie gras. Keep this in mind when choosing a wine to accompany foie gras. A good guideline is always to match high acidity with high acidity.

Because it is often placed first in a line-up of courses, foie gras is commonly paired with Chardonnay or champagne. French champagne is likely to have a higher level of acidity than any wine save those from Germany, and although there are exceptions, white Burgundy is likely to have a higher acidity than other Chardonnays. Certain garnishes may make Chardonnay or champagne attractive at times, but these wines will have a greater affinity with a foie gras mousse or terrine. When considering champagne, only the richer, full-bodied or yeasty styles will be suited to sautéed foie gras.

Those with a compulsion for foie gras will know that ecstatic splendor of experiencing it with wines of dessert-level sweetness. Yet for some, there is a natural reluctance to indulge in such richness at the start of a long meal. Today, foie gras as a starter course is almost the rule, but traditionally it was served at various intervals in the meal. Foie gras actually works well with wines having a wide range of residual sugar levels, allowing plenty of room for experimentation. Once you have arrived at a good match, evaluate the combination of sweetness and richness to determine where in the meal you would like to serve the course. On an empty stomach there is usually less time for the leisurely savoring of foie gras, and depending on the garnish, you may want to reconsider whether or not this is how your meal should begin. Compare the richness of foie gras to that of a cheese course at the end of a meal. A contented appetite induces a slower, more pensive eating, while the fat of the cheese adds a satisfying touch to the meal. A similar approach—foie gras placed after the entrée and served with a high-quality sweet wine—will provide that same sense of luxury and satisfaction. Sauternes, of course, but also Riesling Auslese, Beerenauslese, or Trockenbeerenauslese and late harvest wines of any varietal are all possible choices.

When venturing into sweet wines served other than at the end of a meal, time is an important factor. Sweet wine will impede the appreciation of the drier wines to follow and is problematic in situations where courses arrive in rapid succession without time for the palate to recoup. A wonderful compromise when serving foie gras as an opener would be a demi-sec champagne, as would other lightly sweet sparkling wines from Vouvray, California, or Italy. With the proper approach, residual sugar at these levels need not be detrimental to the palate. To keep up the pace of a meal, salad or consommé will provide a nice palate-cleansing interim course.

Although unadorned foie gras and red wine don't show a great affinity for one another, such a possibility should not be overlooked. Particularly when foie gras is served hot and garnished with a fruit-based sauce as a middle course, Bordeaux and other Cabernet or Merlot wines, and also Pinot Noir, are often quite remarkable pairings. One should be cautioned, however, against wines with too pronounced an oakiness.

Foie Gras with Balsamic Vinegar

SERVES 4

4 ½-inch slices raw grade A
or B foie gras
Flour for dusting
2 tablespoons plus 2
teaspoons balsamic vinegar
4 tablespoons duck
demi-glace
4 teaspoons unsalted butter
Pinch of salt and pepper

The trick to sautéing foie gras is very rapid cooking over a high flame. You want a nice brown crust and rosy interior. Usually, no fat is added to the pan because the foie gras will exude its own fat. Have a drop of olive oil ready, though, because occasionally this does not happen and the foie gras will need a little help. This recipe is nice served with a few mild greens, such as mâche or young spinach, for a garnish.

1   Heat a 10-inch sauté pan until very hot. You will know it is hot enough when a drop of water evaporates immediately.

2   Lightly dust the foie gras with the flour.

3   Add the foie gras to the dry pan. Brown on one side about 10 seconds, and turn over to brown the second side.

4   Remove from the pan immediately to two warm plates.

5   Wipe the pan dry and deglaze with the balsamic vinegar. Add the demi-glace, butter, salt, and pepper and boil to emulsify the butter. Pour over the foie gras and serve.

Balsamic vinegar, found in a broad range of styles and levels of quality, is derived from a complicated series of barrel aging. Yet even the affordable and mass-produced vinegar from Modena, Italy, possesses the almost sweet, woody character for which it is famous. This presents a situation that almost insists on a sweet wine. A Chardonnay that has been barrel-fermented or a nice full champagne with a toasty oakiness will prove detrimental to both food and wine. Combining the oak of a wine with the wood-aged character that is so pronounced in the vinegar will ultimately mask the fruit of even the fullest-bodied wines. With a variety of sweet wine, on the other hand, this preparation can be served at either the beginning or the end of the meal. A Moscato d'Asti from Italy, for example, exhibits the tropical fruit flavors of papaya, mango, and pineapple, and really brings the dish to an exciting new level. If a wine is well made, the acidity will prevent the wine and the foie gras from finishing too sweet. For further discussion, see Wine with Foie Gras, page 82.

Foie Gras with Figs and Red Wine

SERVES 2

2 large, fresh figs

1/3 cup duck stock

1/4 cup red wine

1/2 teaspoon sugar (optional)

Salt and pepper to taste

2 1/3-inch slices grade A or B foie gras

Flour for dusting

1   Cut one of the figs in eight pieces. Cut the other in quarters, lengthwise.

2   In a noncorrosive 1½-quart saucepan, combine the stock, red wine, the fig cut in eight pieces, and the sugar. (If your figs are exceptionally sweet, you may omit the sugar.) Bring to a boil, lower the heat to a simmer, and reduce by half.

3   Pass the sauce through a strainer, pressing through as much of the fig pulp as possible. Return the sauce to the pot.

4   Continue reducing the sauce to a light saucelike consistency. Season with salt and pepper. Place the quartered fig in the sauce and gently heat through. Divide the sauce between two warm plates and place two poached fig pieces on each. Keep warm.

5   Heat a 10-inch skillet over high heat until it is hot enough to evaporate a drop of water immediately. Lightly dust the foie gras with the flour and add to the dry pan. Sprinkle with salt and quickly brown one side, about 10 seconds. Turn over to brown the other side. Place the foie gras on the sauce and serve.

The poached figs in this recipe will provide a wonderful context for sampling different red wines. Since a wide range of red wines will work—such as Bordeaux and other Cabernets and Merlots—the decision should be guided by personal preference. Increased oakiness, leather, clay, or other earthy flavors that often characterize these wines will impress different palates in different ways. Pinot Noir has a slight hint of underlying sweetness to its fruit that has a very subtle relationship with foie gras. You are likely to find that the prettier, more fragrant versions of all these varietals are better suited than the wines that are bigger and heavily oaked. Other interesting regions to sample are those of Madiran or Cahors, neighboring the regions of Gascony and Périgord. Traditionally these are big, heavy, and oaky wines, but lighter versions are currently being shipped to the United States. These deeply flavored red wines will provide essential but uncomplicated fruit that blends nicely with the foie gras. For further discussion, see Wine with Foie Gras, page 82.

Foie Gras and Lobster Salad

SERVES 4

4 ounces raw foie gras,
preferably grade A

½ cup brandy

1 cup Sauternes

2 teaspoons salt

1 (1¼-pound) live lobster

½ cup olive oil

2 tablespoons white wine
vinegar

Salt to taste

2 tablespoons cucumber, cut
into small dice

2 tablespoons green beans,
lightly blanched, and cut into
small dice

2 tablespoons peeled and
seeded tomato, cut into
small dice

2 tablespoons red radish, cut
into small dice

Foie gras and lobster have a wonderful affinity for one another. Paired as they are in this salad, each can be appreciated separately and for the delicious combination they make. The cool, crunchy salad of diced vegetables refreshes the palate between bites of the rich foie gras and lobster meat.

1 Clean the foie gras according to the directions on page 26. Marinate the foie gras in the brandy, Sauternes, and the 2 teaspoons salt for 24 hours, refrigerated.

2 Remove foie gras from the marinade and wrap it four times around with cheesecloth and tie with string. In a noncorrosive saucepan, bring the marinating liquid to a boil. If there is not enough liquid to cover the foie gras, add water.

3 Lower the liquid to a simmer and add the foie gras. Poach for approximately 10–12 minutes, depending on the thickness of the foie gras. A skewer inserted into the center of the liver should come out just slightly warm.

4 Remove the foie gras from the liquid. Place it between two plates and weight lightly. Chill in the refrigerator for at least four hours.

5 Cook the lobster in boiling, salted water for 7 minutes. Remove and cool in cold water. Break off the tail, claws, and a few of the legs. Discard the rest.

6   Crack the claws with a cleaver and remove the meat as neatly as you can. With sharp scissors, cut lengthwise down the underside of the tail and remove the meat.

7   Using a cleaver, chop the lobster shells and legs into 1-inch pieces.

8   Place the olive oil and lobster shells in an 8-inch skillet. Over very low heat, sweat the shells for about one half hour, until the oil turns orange. Drain the oil well and reserve. Discard the shells.

9   Combine the vinegar, the cooled lobster oil, and a pinch of salt. Toss with the diced vegetables.

To serve: Unwrap the foie gras and slice ¼-inch thick. Slice the lobster into bite-size pieces. Divide the vegetable salad among four plates and arrange the foie gras and lobster around it.

Lobster does well with big Chardonnays primarily because of the butter that usually accompanies it—otherwise you are likely to want a crisper and more subdued wine, which is not likely to have an affinity for the more demanding consistency of the poached foie gras. Brut champagne may stand up to some people's taste, but probably through sheer power rather than finesse. A demi-sec champagne will provide that finesse through an elegant sweetness that is very complementary to both the lobster and the foie gras. The light and refreshing quality of the vegetable salad provides a wonderful balance and palate-cleansing effect with a wine of less residual sugar. With a full-fledged late-harvest wine, the dish becomes almost dessertlike, with two very luxurious ingredients and little to counter all the richness. For further discussion, see Wine with Foie Gras, page 82.

Foie Gras with Apples

1   Heat the olive oil in a 10-inch skillet. Sauté the apple slices until browned, turning once, about 5 minutes. Remove to four warmed plates and keep warm.

2   Heat a 10-inch skillet until it is hot enough to evaporate a drop of water immediately. Lightly dust the foie gras with the flour and add to the pan. Sprinkle with salt and quickly brown the first side, about 10 seconds. Turn and brown the other side. Remove to the plates with the apple.

3   Wipe the pan dry and deglaze with the wine. Reduce by half and add the cider, demi-glace, and butter. Reduce until a sauce-like consistency is achieved. Season with salt and pepper and pour over the foie gras.

This fresh fruit and cider garnish doesn't really offer the richness or body usually required for a foie gras and red wine match. The character of the fruit makes white wine the preferred accompaniment. Crisp and very dry Chardonnay, champagne, and Tokay work very well. A moderate barrel fermentation is fine, but in those Chardonnays where oakiness is very pronounced, the wood does not harmonize with the rest of the flavors. For further discussion, see Wine with Foie Gras, page 82.

Foie Gras Terrines

Terrines are probably the best way to experience the delicacy and beauty of foie gras. When they are served chilled, one can linger over them, appreciating the silken texture, the gentle sweetness, the singular aroma, the pure complexion.

Foie gras gives itself to a variety of flavorings and enhancements, each chosen to augment the liver's natural goodness. Additions to a terrine can also create a colorful or variegated mosaic.

Terrines get their name simply from the vessel in which they are baked or molded. These containers can be of many shapes, but are usually rectangular or oval and most often made of porcelain, earthenware, tin, or enameled cast iron. If the presentation calls for even, regular slices, a rectangular terrine is required, preferably a heavy one made of enameled cast iron. Such a terrine distributes the heat evenly and will not discolor the foie gras.

There are two basic ways to make a foie gras terrine—either by gently baking whole livers directly in the terrine or by using the terrine to chill and mold a foie gras mousse. There are advantages to both these techniques, depending upon the desired result. In either case, you must first decide on a marinade. Sweet wines, such as Sauternes, Pineau des Charentes, Riesling, and Port are all good choices and will enhance the sweetness of the liver. Other white wines and brandy are also used, often in combination. For whole liver terrines, salt is an essential element of the marinade, and plenty of it. There must be enough to penetrate the liver, to both season it and draw out the blood—an undersalted foie gras terrine tastes bland.

Most whole liver terrines will require two foie gras, but this really depends on the size of both the liver and the mold. A grade A foie gras is best for this preparation, as it is larger and less veiny. After cleaning and marinating, you can add extra flavorings by coating the outside of the foie gras, using crushed peppercorns, chopped black truffles (which have a special affinity for foie gras), or roasted garlic, for example. Lightly grease the inside of the terrine itself with duck fat or butter to get the coating to stick. You can also create a beautiful mosaic by interspersing precooked vegetables set lengthwise among the liver lobes. After a slow baking, the light weight placed on the terrine will gently press everything together, molding the foie gras around the vegetables. After it is chilled, the foie gras will become firm and crosswise slices will reveal your pattern.

Foie gras mousse terrines have the advantage of economy and pliability. You can use a less expensive, grade B liver, and the addition of cream and butter means you'll use less foie gras to make a terrine. It is important not to use too much cream and butter, however, so as not to mask the foie gras taste. The mousse can then be layered in the terrine with a wide variety of complementary items. Cooked duck meat, prosciutto, duck liver mousse, lobster, avocado mousse, and aspic are all possibilities. When chilled and sliced, the even layers of varying colors and textures can be stunning.

Garnishes should be cool and palate-cleansing, such as pickled vegetables or a little lightly dressed salad. Aspic is also a classic accompaniment, which can be infused with many flavors, such as ginger or port. And of course, some warm toast, possibly brioche, is a must.

Tip: It is best to use a very sharp knife with a long, thin blade to slice foie gras terrine. Heat the knife blade under hot water and wipe it dry before slicing—it will glide through the terrine much more easily. (Do not heat the blade for terrines in which aspic has been incorporated—the heat will melt the aspic.)

Foie Gras, Avocado, and Aspic Terrine

This is a very elegant and beautiful terrine to serve as a prelude to a formal sit-down dinner. Serve it garnished with grated turnip dressed with a little white wine vinegar, salt, and white pepper.

To Prepare the Foie Gras Mousse

1   Clean the foie gras according to the directions on page 26. In a 1½-quart pot of simmering salted water, gently poach the foie gras for approximately 10 minutes, or until a skewer inserted into the center of the liver comes out slightly warm. Remove the foie gras from the water and refrigerate until chilled.

2   Cut the chilled foie gras into 1-inch pieces and place in a food processor. Process 10 seconds. Add the cream all at once and process another 20 seconds.

3   Slowly add the melted butter, watching to see it is incorporated. Stop adding butter if the mousse looks like it is not absorbing any more and might curdle. Process until smooth. Do not overprocess or it will curdle.

4   Scrape the contents of the processor into a bowl. Season with the salt, pepper, and port. Cover with plastic wrap and have ready at room temperature.

SERVES APPROXIMATELY 20

FOR THE FOIE GRAS MOUSSE
8 ounces raw grade B foie gras
½ cup heavy cream
4 tablespoons unsalted butter, melted and cooled to room temperature
Salt and white pepper, to taste
2 teaspoons port

FOR THE AVOCADO MOUSSE
1½ teaspoons unflavored gelatin
½ cup heavy cream
2 ripe Haas avocados
Salt and white pepper, to taste

ALSO
2 cups duck aspic, melted and at room temperature (see page 25)

To Prepare the Avocado Mousse

1 In a bowl, dissolve the gelatin in 1 tablespoon cold water. Let sit 3 minutes.

2 Bring the cream to a boil and pour it over the gelatin, whisking until combined.

3 Peel the avocadoes and cut them into 1-inch chunks. Place these in the bowl of a food processor or blender. Puree the avocado, adding the hot cream mixture in a stream.

4 Remove the avocado mixture to a bowl and season with salt and pepper. Press plastic wrap directly onto the surface of the mousse to prevent browning and keep it covered at all times.

To Assemble the Terrine

1 In a 5-cup terrine, pour ½ cup of aspic. Place in the refrigerator to set, about 20 minutes.

2 On top of the set aspic, evenly spread a ¼-inch layer of foie gras mousse. It is worth taking the time to be careful and do this evenly and neatly because it will improve the appearance of the finished terrine. Place in the refrigerator to set, about 20 minutes.

3 On top of the set foie gras, evenly spread a ¼-inch layer of avocado mousse. Add another layer of aspic, pouring it gently onto the avocado over the back of a spoon. Place in the refrigerator to set, about 20 minutes.

4 Continue layering the rest of the ingredients in this way, finishing with a layer of aspic. Let the terrine set in the refrigerator for at least 8 hours.

5   To unmold, place the terrine briefly in a hot water bath to loosen the aspic. Invert onto a platter. Slice with a thin, sharp knife.

This will keep for at least one week in the refrigerator. The avocado will brown slightly around the edges after a day, but this may be trimmed off.

Although still highly sensuous with sweeter wines, foie gras in this form will be more compatable with dry Chardonnays and champagne. The cream and butter in the mousse serve to mellow the intensity of the foie gras and allow for a smoother blending of its flavors with the wine. Butter and cream will, to an extent, allow a greater amount of oak to enter the flavor combination, but at a certain point the wood flavors tend to stand separate and begin to taste rather harsh and out of balance.

Foie Gras Terrine with Port Aspic

SERVES
APPROXIMATELY 15

2 raw grade A foie gras
¾ cup brandy
2 cups Sauternes
1 tablespoon kosher salt
1½ cups duck consommé
½ cup port
Salt to taste
1 package unflavored gelatin

This terrine is made from the whole foie gras gently cooked and weighted in a terrine mold, then chilled and sliced before serving. The port aspic makes a wonderful garnish, but there are many other garnishes that would be appropriate, such as a little salad, some marinated radish or raw turnip, and certainly some good toast. The idea is to provide a crisp, cool-tasting palate cleanser to enjoy between bites of the terrine. This recipe is for a small terrine, which is more practical for most people. If you would like to prepare a larger one, the technique is the same. A grade A foie gras is preferred because it is less veiny and makes a better presentation (see page 8).

1   Clean the foie gras according to the directions on page 26.

2   Combine the brandy, Sauternes, and salt. The best way to marinate the foie gras is to place it in a resealable plastic bag with the marinade. You can marinate it in a bowl, but you will need more marinade or will have to turn the foie gras every so often. Marinate overnight in the refrigerator.

3   Remove the foie gras from the marinade and pat dry. Fit the pieces into a 4-cup terrine. Cover with foil, set in a water bath, and bake in a 250° oven for about 30 minutes. You will know the foie gras is done when a skewer inserted into the center comes out warm. The foie gras will also have become very loose and jiggly. It is very important not to overcook the terrine—it will seem underdone if you haven't done this before.

4   Remove the terrine from the water bath and place a weight of a few pounds on it while it cools to room temperature. This will compact the foie gras into the shape of the terrine and cause the lobes to adhere to each other. You will have to be creative with what you have in your house to find a weight of the proper size and heaviness—a full box of kosher salt works well if your terrine is the right size. Don't overweight it, or you will smash the foie gras.

5   When the terrine is room temperature, refrigerate it overnight. To unmold, dip the terrine very briefly in a hot water bath to loosen the surrounding fat, and invert onto a platter.

6   While the terrine is cooking, prepare the aspic. Bring the consommé to a boil. Season with the port and salt.

7   Place the gelatin in a bowl. Add 3 tablespoons cold water and let stand 3 minutes. Add the hot consommé to this and stir to dissolve the gelatin completely.

8   There are several ways to present the aspic. You can pour the hot aspic into a flat shallow dish, refrigerate it, then cut out shapes, and you can chill it in any shaped container and then chop it up fine. Another alternative is to lightly coat the bottom of your appetizer plate with the aspic, let it set, and serve your terrine on top of it. Any way is beautiful, but be sure to use well-chilled plates so the aspic doesn't melt.

9   Be very careful when handling the terrine, always keeping it on a flat, even surface. Too much handling will cause the lobes to separate and make it difficult to slice. This terrine will keep, well wrapped, for at least a week.

This terrine will be less conducive to pairing with dry white wines or champagne than the foie gras terrine with avocado and aspic, page 93. Not only is it lacking the butter and cream that would mellow the intensity of the liver, but there are also two elements of sweetness included in the preparation—the Sauternes and the port. Although not in direct conflict, most dry wines will not show their best next to the marinade of Sauternes and the subtle sweetness that is contained in the port aspic. This is problematic in that these ingredients provide subtle adornment to the foie gras that a more forceful wine can easily disrupt. A well-made Chenin Blanc, or a sparkling wine with just a slight level of classy sweetness balanced with a good acidity, ought to fit this type of terrine very nicely.

ENTRÉES

Working with a whole duck in the context of the entrée, it would be difficult to conceive of a preparation that made full use of all parts. Every time duck is served as a main course, there will be parts and by-products on hand to use in soups, salads, stock, sauces, confit, and more. Only through experience and experimentation will you come to understand the full extent of its economy and versatility, which will, in turn, inspire you to include duck in your weekly menu planning. To enhance that inspiration, here are some entrée ideas adapted from culinary traditions around the world.

Ballottine with Spinach and Pinenuts

4–8 SERVINGS

4 cups fresh spinach, packed
1 small shallot, peeled and finely chopped
1/2 teaspoon finely chopped garlic
1/2 teaspoon kosher salt
1/4 teaspoon freshly ground pepper
1/2 cup fresh breadcrumbs
Juice of half a lemon
1/4 teaspoon dry tarragon
1/2 cup toasted pine nuts
1 5-pound Pekin or Muscovy duck, boned according to method 1 on page 18

*T*his ballottine makes a lovely luncheon dish as well as a fine dinner. Here it is made with a spinach filling, but you can vary the stuffing as you wish. A pâté filling is particularly nice, especially with a nugget of foie gras in the center. It may be served cold with an herb vinaigrette (see page 42) or hot with a Madeira sauce (see page 36).

1   Steam the spinach using only the water left clinging to the leaves after washing. Let cool, squeeze dry, and chop coarsely.

2   In a bowl, combine the spinach, shallot, garlic, salt, pepper, breadcrumbs, lemon juice, tarragon, and pine nuts. Mix thoroughly.

3   Lay the duck out flat, skin side down. Remove the breasts, carefully separating them from the skin. With the smooth side of a meat pounder, flatten the breasts somewhat, so that they will cover more of the duck skin.

4   Remove any excess fat from the duck, especially from around the legs. Lay the breasts back in their original position, covering as much skin as possible. Lightly sprinkle with salt and pepper.

5   Spread the spinach mixture evenly and thoroughly over the duck. Carefully roll up the duck to form a cylinder—try not to roll the skin into the interior of the ballottine. Smooth the ends over and tie the duck with butcher's twine at 1-inch intervals. Do not tie too tightly—the duck will plump as it roasts. Sprinkle with salt and pepper.

6   Place the duck on a rack set in a roasting pan and roast in a 350° oven for 45 minutes to 1 hour, or until the skin is browned and crisp and a skewer inserted into the center of the ballottine comes out hot. If the ballottine is not browning enough, raise the oven temperature to 425° for the last 10–15 minutes.

7   If the ballottine is to be served hot, let it rest for 5 minutes, then untie and slice into ½-inch pieces. For a cold ballottine, cool at room temperature and then cover and refrigerate. Let it come to a cool room temperature before serving.

This preparation is worth the effort, as it provides an experience that is quite unlike that of simple roasted duck. First, the meat is cooked off the bone, giving it a lighter, less gamy character, and secondly, the process includes pounding out the meat, which tenderizes it. The ballottine with herb vinaigrette is an excellent staple for a summertime buffet. For such a situation red wines such as Beaujolais, or lighter Pinot Noir or Chianti could be served chilled with a pleasant effect. Some palates may have difficulty, however, with the manner in which the flavors of the spinach and herbs blend with most red wines. The fruit of a very lush and full-bodied Chardonnay is far more compatible with the pine nuts and herbal elements, demonstrating that the mild and tender duck meat is well suited to white wines. Oaky wines are unintrusive and may be a matter of preference. Sancerre and probably all Sauvignon Blanc should be avoided. Attempting to combine the herbs in the ballottine and herbacious wine results in an unpleasant clash. For gatherings in cooler weather see Madeira Sauce, page 36.

Duck Cannelloni with Red Wine Sauce and Crispy Shallots

SERVES 4

FOR THE FILLING
2 duck legs
1 duck liver, finely chopped
½ cup red wine
1 shallot, finely chopped
2 cloves garlic, finely chopped
½ cup duck demi-glace
Kosher salt and pepper,
to taste

FOR THE SAUCE
¾ cup red wine
1½ cups duck demi-glace
Kosher salt and pepper,
to taste
1 tablespoon unsalted butter

Made with homemade pasta, these cannelloni are surprisingly light although deep in flavor. Use a good-quality wine with a dry-style fruit for the sauce.

1   Roast the duck legs in a 400° oven until done, about 45 minutes. Remove and let cool.

2   While the duck is roasting, prepare the pasta dough according to the directions on page 79. Let rest in the refrigerator, covered with plastic, for one hour.

3   When the duck is cool enough to handle, remove and discard all skin and bones. Using two forks, shred the duck meat. Place the duck in a bowl and add the duck liver.

4   In a 1½-quart saucepan or a small skillet, combine the wine with the shallot and garlic and reduce by half. Add the demi-glace and reduce to ¼ cup. Let cool.

5   Add the reduction to the duck and toss. There should be just enough to moisten the meat. Season with salt and pepper.

6 Prepare the sauce. In a 1½-quart saucepan, reduce the wine to ¼ cup. Add the demi-glace and reduce to 1 cup or until a saucelike consistency has been achieved. Season with salt and pepper to taste. When ready to serve, take the hot red wine sauce off the stove and swirl in the butter.

7 While the sauce is reducing, prepare the cannelloni. Roll the pasta out into thin sheets according to the manufacturer's directions for your pasta machine. Keep the remaining pasta covered with plastic wrap or a damp towel while you work.

8 If using a cannelloni mold, flour it lightly. Lay a sheet of pasta on it. Brush all the borders lightly but thoroughly with the beaten egg. Fill the cannelloni with the duck mixture. Lay another sheet of pasta on top and press gently with the palms of your hands to express any air and to seal. Roll across the top of the mold with a rolling pin to seal and cut out the cannelloni. Repeat with the remaining dough and filling. Keep the finished cannelloni on a floured board or plate, spaced so they are not touching.

9 Cook the cannelloni in boiling, salted water for 2–3 minutes, until al dente. Drain and cool under cold water.

10 If not using a cannelloni mold, cook the sheets of pasta whole in boiling, salted water for 1–2 minutes, until al dente. Drain and cool under cold water. Dry the pasta by blotting it with paper towels. Cut the pasta sheets into 5-inch squares. Roll the duck mixture in the squares, leaving the ends open.

11 Place the cannelloni on a buttered sheet pan. Cover with aluminum foil and heat in a 350° oven until thoroughly hot and slightly browned on the bottom, about 10 minutes.

ALSO
1 recipe Pasta Dough
(see page 79)
Flour for dusting
1 egg, beaten
½ cup vegetable oil
4 large shallots, cut in half
and thinly sliced lengthwise

12 While the cannelloni are in the oven, heat the vegetable oil in a 10-inch skillet. In batches, fry the shallots until browned. Drain on paper towels and sprinkle with salt. They will get crisper as they cool.

13 To serve, place the cannelloni on a plate and top with the sauce and fried shallots.

Cannelloni works well as a middle or main course with medium-bodied, but deeply flavored, red wines. Although the liver is a very minor element in the recipe and its flavors are subtle, they are major for a red wine to overcome. The livery, gamy quality of the meat in the cannelloni is complemented by the crispy shallots, which add a hint of sweetness to the red wine reduction sauce. Specific varietal character is needed to balance the earthy flavors of the filling, but any lushness of fruit will prove overbearing and almost sweet because of the shallots and red wine reduction.

The sauce will provide the dish with a pretty high acidity, so a good acidity should be considered when selecting the wine. Brunello di Montalcino or other rossos based on the Sangiovese Grosso, and bigger-bodied Chianti Classicos, provide a deep concentration of flavor and have the dryness in the character of their fruit that is key to a successful match here.

Roast Duck with Fettuccine, Mushrooms, and Herbs

SERVES 2–4

1 5-pound Pekin duck
Kosher salt and pepper,
to taste
1 medium onion, cut into
1-inch pieces
1 carrot, cut into 1-inch pieces
1 small bunch sage
1 small bunch thyme
1 small bunch parsley
4 strips double-smoked bacon,
cut into ½-inch pieces
2 cups sliced mushrooms
¼ cup chopped shallots
1 cup red wine
1 quart duck stock
Fresh fettuccine (see page 79),
cooked

This recipe is written for Pekin duck, but obviously you may substitute a Muscovy here.

1   Preheat the oven to 300°

2   Remove the wing tips and any extra fat from the duck. Reserve for another use. Rinse the duck and pat dry. Sprinkle the cavity with salt and pepper. Place the onion, carrot, a few sprigs of the sage, thyme, and parsley, and a few pieces of the bacon into the cavity of the duck.

3   Place the duck, breast side down, on a roasting rack set in a roasting pan and roast for ½ hour.

4   Turn the duck breast side up. Increase the temperature to 350°, and continue roasting for 1½ hours.

5   Increase the heat again to 450° and roast approximately 45 minutes longer until the duck is golden brown and crisp. Individual ovens will vary, so adjust the temperature if the duck is browning too quickly.

6   Remove from the oven and let rest 5 minutes before carving.

7   While the duck is roasting, sauté the remaining bacon in a 10-inch skillet until crisp. Remove and reserve. Pour off all but 1 tablespoon of the bacon fat.

8   Over high heat, sauté the mushrooms in the bacon fat until browned. Lower the flame to medium, add the shallots, and cook for 2 minutes. Remove the contents of the pan to the bacon and reserve.

9   Return the pan to the stove and deglaze with the red wine. Reduce to approximately ¼ cup. Add the stock, bring to a boil, and reduce until a light saucelike consistency is achieved, about 10 minutes.

10   While the sauce is reducing, coarsely chop the remaining herbs. When it is reduced enough, add the herbs, mushrooms, shallots, and bacon. Season with salt and pepper to taste. When you are ready to serve, gently toss the fettuccine in the sauce to heat and combine.

11   To serve, carve the duck (see page 20). Place fettuccine and sauce on individual plates and surround with duck meat. Haricot vert and a peppery watercress salad dressed with balsamic vinaigrette make good accompaniments.

This red wine– and duck stock–based sauce, with its earthy and smoky overtones from bacon and sautéed mushrooms, is pleasantly matched with a well-aged, full-flavored Barolo or Barbaresco. More easily attainable would be an Inferno or a variety of Nebbiolo-based wines from Piedmont and the neighboring regions of northern Italy. Although lacking some of the majestic character of the wines from the more famous regions, many of these very affordable wines possess the same strong, aggressive flavors and pungent truffle aromas that blend wonderfully with this sauce. Most will be full bodied enough to be complemented by the succulence of the duck meat.

Fuller-bodied Pinot Noir and Zinfandel maintain a nice affinity with this wonderful blending of flavors, but they should possess a dry rather than a lush style of fruit.

Pan-Fried Noodles with Duck, Ginger, and Scallions

SERVES 2

FOR THE NOODLES

2 tablespoons vegetable oil

12 ounces thin Chinese egg noodles precooked (or substitute angel hair pasta)

FOR THE DUCK

1½ teaspoons vegetable oil

2 skinless duck breasts, thinly sliced crosswise

2 teaspoons grated ginger

2 cloves garlic, finely chopped

2 teaspoons soy sauce

1 cup duck demi-glace

2 scallions, thinly sliced

Salt and pepper, to taste

1½ teaspoons cornstarch, dissolved in 1 tablespoon cold water

1 In a 12-inch skillet, heat the 2 tablespoons of vegetable oil until very hot. Divide the noodles in half and make two piles in the pan. Flatten each one to form a pancake about ¾-inch thick. Lower the heat to moderate and cook, shaking the pan occasionally, until golden brown. Flip and brown the other side. Add more oil to the pan if necessary.

2 While the noodles are cooking, heat the 1½ teaspoons of vegetable oil in a 10-inch skillet until it is very hot and begins to smoke. Add the duck breast, ginger, and garlic, and quickly brown the meat, stirring for 30 seconds.

3 Add the soy sauce, demi-glace, scallions, salt, and pepper. Cook 1 minute.

4 Add the cornstarch mixture and heat until thickened.

5 Place the noodle pancakes on two plates. Surround with the duck and sauce. Serve with some braised bok choy or steamed snow peas.

Because of the potent blending of flavors, this dish calls for an uncomplicated white wine with a substantial acidity. A French Muscadet would provide a nice crisp and clean accompaniment, or a Chenin Blanc with a slight sweetness would also be suitable. The flavor of soy sauce is potent next to most wines and adds to the saltiness of the dish. The saltiness will also have an accentuating effect on the alcohol, possibly throwing things out of balance. In this case, an affordable Riesling is the answer; the stronger character of the grape and the generally lower alcohol content found in these wines address this conflict.

Duck with Olives

SERVES 2–4

1 teaspoon olive oil

Legs and breast of a 5-pound
Pekin, or 4 duck legs

3 cloves garlic, finely chopped

1 cup medium-diced onion

1 tablespoon blanched
medium-diced slab bacon

1½ cups red wine

1 quart duck stock

1 teaspoon dry thyme

1 bay leaf

¾ cup Moroccan oil-cured
olives and Kalamata olives
combined, pitted, and cut into
large pieces

Pepper to taste

For this recipe, we use both black Moroccan oil-cured olives and the tangier Kalamata. Other imported olives may be substituted, but these varieties complement each other nicely and add a beautiful deep, dark, purple-black color to the stew.

1   Heat the olive oil in a heavy-bottomed 3-quart saucepan. Over medium heat, brown the duck on all sides.

2   Remove the duck and pour off all but 1 tablespoon of the rendered fat.

3   Add the garlic, onion, and bacon and sauté lightly, about 5 minutes, until the onion is translucent.

4   Return the duck to the pot, along with the red wine. Reduce the wine by half, about 10 minutes.

5   Add the stock, thyme, and bay leaf, and bring to a boil over high heat. Reduce the flame to keep the stew at a slow simmer.

6   Simmer 45 minutes. Then add the olives and simmer another 30 minutes, until the duck is meltingly tender. Season to taste with pepper.

The powerful and assertive flavors of Kalamata and Morroccan olives are a very commanding part of this dish and require a very strong-flavored wine to accompany it. The character of the fruit in the red wines of Portugal might come as a shock to the uninitiated, but you will find that their intenseness of flavor will parallel that of even the strongest olives. The Bordeaux from Pauillac and St. Estephe also show well with this dish. The wines of Bordeaux and Portugal are stylistically very different and may well affect the manner in which the dish is prepared. The hearty and more rustic Portuguese wines are well suited to a presentation with an abundance of very coarsely chopped olives. On the other hand, this country-style preparation might prove to be inappropriate for the more refined nature of the Bordeaux. Although the character of the fruit blends ideally, too much olive can overwhelm the wines' more elegant subtleties. When you uncork a fine Bordeaux, not only are very finely chopped olives a more effective combination, but the dish appears more delicate visually and better suited for the occasion.

Also certain to work well on a traditional level are a variety of wines from the Rhône region or Provence, where olives are integral to the cuisine. You will find a wide variance in the pricing of these wines as well as many variations in the blending of the local varietals. Here again, either the hearty and rustic or the very refined styles of wine from these regions will work effectively. However, like the Bordeaux, a well-aged Châteauneuf-du-Pape, for instance, is in danger of having some of its subtleties buried by an abundance of olives.

Duck Gumbo

SERVES 2–4

2 slices bacon, cut into ¼-inch pieces

1 5-pound Pekin duck, quartered

Vegetable oil, as needed

¼ cup flour

1 rib celery, coarsely chopped

1 small red pepper, seeded and coarsely chopped

1 small green pepper, seeded and coarsely chopped

3 scallions, coarsely chopped

1 medium onion, coarsely chopped

5 cloves garlic, peeled and coarsely chopped

⅓ cup diced smoked ham

2 teaspoons kosher salt

1 teaspoon dry thyme

1 teaspoon cayenne

1 teaspoon freshly ground black pepper

2 bay leaves

1 quart duck stock

1 teaspoon gumbo filé*

Gumbo is one of the quintessential American dishes. With duck hunting so popular in Louisiana, it seemed fitting to include this recipe. There are as many variations on this dish as there are cooks. To make it a gumbo, however, you must include either gumbo filé, which is powdered sassafras, or okra. Crackling Biscuits (see page 176) and rice are great accompaniments.

1   In a heavy-bottomed, 3½-quart casserole, fry the bacon until crisp. Remove with a slotted spoon and reserve. Add the duck pieces and brown on all sides. Remove the duck and reserve.

2   Pour off all but ¼ cup of the fat. If there is not ¼ cup, add some vegetable oil to the pot. Add the flour all at once to make a roux. Over a medium heat, keep whisking the flour until it is a dark reddish brown, a little darker than peanut butter.

3   Add the chopped vegetables, along with the ham and all the seasonings, to the roux. This will stop the roux from getting any darker. Stir the vegetables frequently and cook them until they start to give off juices and get soft, about 10–15 minutes.

4   Add the stock, the browned duck pieces, and the reserved bacon and bring to a boil. Lower to a simmer and cook for about 1 hour and 15 minutes, skimming occasionally, until the duck is tender. Turn off the heat, add the gumbo filé powder, and stir to combine thoroughly.

Tip: It is best to make this gumbo a few days ahead to allow the flavors to age. If doing so, do not add the filé until ready to serve.

---

* Gumbo filé is available in most specialty food shops.

Gumbo is associated with heavily spiced Louisiana and Cajun cuisines. As in many classic foods with potent spice, we have here the contrasting element of sweet vegetables, which adds to the complexity of the gumbo. The degree of spice will affect your choice of wine, although the dish may be crying out for an ice cold beer. Riesling and Gewürtztraminer, both sweet and dry, are the only varietals with powerful enough flavor to stand up to the intensity of this gumbo. Gewürtztraminer is the more likely to be overwhelmed by the spice, although with a lighter hand on the pepper, its spicy fruit meshes very well with the sweetness of the vegetables and really adds a level of complexity to the dish. Riesling, on the other hand, has the intensity of fruit to stand up to a spicier recipe, and the power of the fruit is forward enough to act as a coolant on the palate.

Thai Duck Stew with Red Curry

SERVES 4

1 5-pound Pekin duck with legs, thighs, boneless breasts, and wings separated

1 tablespoon vegetable oil

2 teaspoons Thai red curry paste

1 tablespoon chopped garlic

5 (¼-inch) slices fresh ginger

2 teaspoons sugar

7 Kaffir lime leaves

1 quart duck stock

3 tablespoons Thai fish sauce

1 medium onion, halved and cut lengthwise into ¼-inch slices

1 medium zucchini, quartered lengthwise and cut crosswise into ½-inch pieces

1 (14-ounce) can straw mushrooms, drained

Juice of two limes

1 teaspoon Vietnamese hot sauce

1 can unsweetened Thai coconut milk

Duck is used in many Thai recipes, combined with different curries and often barbequed. The Thai combinations of hot-sweet and salty-sweet are very well suited to the character of duck meat. The coconut milk in this recipe adds a sweet balance to the red curry.

1   Preheat the oven to 400°.

2   Roast the duck pieces for 20 minutes to render some of the fat.

3   In a 3½-quart, noncorrosive saucepan, combine the vegetable oil, curry paste, and garlic, and gently sauté over low heat for 5 minutes.

4   Add the drained, roasted duck pieces, reserving the fat for another use. Add the ginger, sugar, lime leaves, stock, and fish sauce. Bring to a boil and lower to a simmer. Cook 1½ hours or until the duck is tender. Skim occasionally and discard the fat that rises to the top.

5   Add the onion, zucchini, straw mushrooms, lime juice, and hot sauce. Simmer another 15 minutes.

6   Add the coconut milk and heat through but do not boil. Adjust the seasonings to taste.

7   Serve as is or over a bowl of rice noodles.

The pungent combination of ginger and garlic in Far Eastern cuisine has long presented a pitfall in wine accompaniment, and this particular dish is further complicated by the acidity of the lime juice. Such acidity must be countered by an equally firm acidity and assertive varietal character in your choice of wine, and you'll find that either dry or off-dry is effective. There is a group of widely overlooked world-class wines that should really be sampled with this dish. They are the Charta wines from the Rheingau region of Germany. The Charta association was founded to ensure that the highest-quality wine would be produced in the Rheingau. The demanding standards set for its members produce wines that appear quite dry on the palate and combine an intensity of fruit with a very well-structured level of acidity. Not only do these wines bear up to the formidable spices of this dish, but they do so with a surprising amount of finesse. The Charta designation indicates a very distinct style of wine, but there are also other wines of superb quality from the Rheingau and other regions of Germany that will blend effectively in this context. Of the drier style, many will be labeled *Spätlese Trocken* —*Trocken* meaning "dry." Although Spätlese is normally a sweeter wine, these are fermented dry, resulting in a higher-than-average alcohol content for German wine, about 11–12 percent. Yet they retain all the richness of fruit normally found in a Spätlese.

Some fruitier Chardonnay wines might also have the potential to stand up to these seasonings, but if there is more than a slight oakiness, they are sure to conflict. For the truly initiated, a dry Gewürztraminer from Alsace will provide a most adventurous combination.

Whole Boneless Duck Stuffed with Sticky Rice

2 ½ cups glutinous rice

4 Chinese duck sausages

¼ cup dried shrimp

1 cup dried shiitake
mushrooms

1 tablespoon soy oil

1 tablespoon grated fresh
ginger

1 tablespoon finely chopped
garlic

1 cup peeled and quartered
waterchestnuts

¼ cup diced duck ham
(optional)

2 scallions, cut into ½-inch
pieces

1 tablespoon fermented fish
sauce

2 tablespoons soy sauce

2 tablespoons Chinese rice
wine or Fino sherry

1 ½ cups duck stock

One 5-pound Pekin duck,
boned (see method two,
page 20)

This is an old-fashioned Chinese dish, sometimes served as part of a banquet or for the New Year's celebration. Sticky rice, sometimes called glutinous or sweet rice, has a wonderful unctuous texture and earthy flavor and is used in many Chinese dishes. This particular stuffing is also sometimes served steamed in lotus leaves for dim sum. Glutinous rice and Chinese duck sausages are both available at Oriental food stores.

1   Soak the glutinous rice at room temperature for 8 hours or overnight in 6 cups cold water. Drain.

2   Steam the sausages for 15 minutes, then slice them on the diagonal into ½-inch pieces.

3   Soak the dried shrimp in warm water for 15 minutes. Drain and coarsely chop.

4   Soak the dried mushrooms in warm water until softened, about 15 minutes. Drain. Remove the stems and discard. Quarter the caps.

5   Heat the soy oil in a large frying pan over medium heat. Add the ginger and garlic and sauté until softened, about 1 minute.

6 Add the waterchestnuts, duck ham, sausages, shrimp, and mushrooms and sauté one minute. Add the scallions, rice, fermented fish sauce, soy sauce, and rice wine or sherry and stir to combine. Add the stock and mix thoroughly. Turn the heat down to low, cover the mixture, and simmer until the rice is softened, about 15–20 minutes. If the liquid is absorbed and the rice is not cooked through, add a little more stock or water, re-cover, and cook a few more minutes.

7 Remove the stuffing from the pan to a bowl and let it cool before stuffing the duck.

8 Fill the duck with the stuffing, pushing it into the wings and legs to fill out the shape. Do not overfill—save any leftover stuffing for a snack. Tuck the neck skin under the duck and smooth the skin around the cavity over the 'stuffing. Tie the ankles together over the opening with a piece of twine.

9 Place the duck on a rack set in a roasting pan and roast in a 350° oven for 1½–2 hours, until crispy. Pour off the fat from the pan occasionally while roasting.

10 Let the duck rest 5 minutes before carving. To carve, place the duck on a serving platter. Cut the duck completely in half lengthwise, then cut crosswise into 2-inch pieces.

Sticky rice has an effect on the palate that requires a fuller red wine to serve as a rinsing agent and to blend with the varying flavors of the stuffing. The Eastern seasonings, normally considered too strong for red wine, acquire a mellower and distinctly different effect after steaming in the roasting duck. The shiitakes and duck sausages add earthiness and seasoned sweetness that work wonderfully with Pinot Noir or a nice full Zinfandel.

Roast Duck with Sage Stuffing

SERVES 2–4

1 5-pound Pekin or Muscovy
duck
1 large Italian bread
3 tablespoons duck fat
3 tablespoons plus
2 teaspoons unsalted butter
1 cup medium-diced onion
2 cloves garlic, finely chopped
1 tablespoon dry thyme
1 tablespoon coarsely chopped
fresh sage
1 egg, beaten
1/3 cup duck stock
Kosher salt and pepper to
taste

1   Preheat the oven to 375°.

2   Trim away any excess skin from the neck of the duck, leaving about 1½ inches. Pull out the fat from the cavity and reserve both the skin and the fat for another use. Rinse the duck and pat dry.

3   Trim the crust from the bread and cut into ½-inch cubes. You will get about 3 cups.

4   In a 10-inch skillet, melt 1 tablespoon duck fat and 1 table-spoon butter over a medium flame. Add 1 cup of bread cubes, tossing to coat them with the fat. Sauté, tossing occasionally, until the croutons are golden. Transfer them to a bowl. Repeat twice more, using the rest of the bread.

5   Wipe the skillet clean. Melt the remaining 2 teaspoons butter over a medium flame and lightly sauté the onion and garlic until translucent and slightly golden. Transfer to the bowl holding the croutons.

6   Add the rest of the stuffing ingredients, salt and pepper to taste, and mix thoroughly. Fill the cavity of the duck with the stuffing mixture.

7   Sprinkle the duck with salt and pepper. Place on a roasting rack in a shallow pan. Roast the duck in the middle of the oven, basting occasionally, for 1 hour and 15 minutes. Turn the oven up to 450° for the last 15 minutes if the duck is not brown enough. Remove from the oven and let rest for 5 minutes.

8   Transfer the stuffing to a serving bowl. Carve the bird (see page 20) and serve. This roast is delicious served with a simple white wine sauce or thyme and sage sauce (page 40).

So you have a priceless red Burgundy that has been aged to perfection in flawless temperature-controlled conditions. Many a wine enthusiast would be insistent on uncorking the bottle and consuming it on its own, to appreciate it for the great masterpiece that it is likely to be without the complications of an elaborate dining situation. This is certainly a legitimate approach to the enjoyment of your investment. However, if you believe that wine is meant to be consumed with a meal, the handling of a very special wine deserves a very conscientious approach to food preparation. When it comes to complementing the unadorned meat of a roasted duck, nothing does better than Pinot Noir. You will find that sage also has a special affinity for this varietal, and the flavors will interweave very subtly on the palate, allowing you to appreciate that special bottle for all its attributes of earth and fruit. The meat can be moistened with the delicate white wine sauce (with or without a sage infusion) and not interfere with the wine to any great extent; refer to the recipe on page 40 before considering other wines to accompany roast duck.

Roast Duck with Cornbread Stuffing

SERVES 2–4

*3 cups cornbread, cut into
1-inch cubes (see page 175)
4 teaspoons unsalted butter
1 cup chopped onion
½ teaspoon dry thyme
1 egg
½–¾ cup duck stock
Kosher salt and pepper, to
taste
1 5-pound Pekin or Muscovy
duck*

1   Place the cornbread cubes in a bowl.

2   Melt the butter in a 6-inch sauté pan. Add the onion and sweat over medium low heat for about 10 minutes until the onion turns translucent. Add the thyme and cook one more minute.

3   Add the contents of the sauté pan to the cornbread. Add the egg, ½ cup of stock, and the salt and pepper. Combine thoroughly. If the stuffing seems too dry, add the remaining stock.

4   Rinse the duck and pat dry. Season with salt and pepper inside and out. Fill the cavity with the stuffing, but don't pack it in too tightly. If there is any extra, you can stuff the neck cavity with it.

5   Place the duck on a rack set in a roasting pan and place in a 375° oven for about 1 hour and 15 minutes, depending on the type of duck. Smaller and leaner ducks will cook faster. You will know it is done when the skin is crispy and a skewer inserted into the stuffing comes out hot. If the duck is not browning enough, raise the temperature to 400° for the last 15 minutes.

6   To serve, remove the stuffing to a bowl. Let the duck rest for 5 minutes then carve (see page 20).

For wine suggestions, see White Wine Sauce (page 40).

Confit

Confit originated in southwestern France as a technique for curing, preserving, and tenderizing meat. The most common meats made into confit are duck, goose, pork, and rabbit. Garlic and shallots can also be prepared in this manner. The process involves dry-marinating the meat in salt, herbs, and spices to both flavor and help preserve it, and then slowly cooking it in its own fat. In the case of meats such as rabbit or lamb, the fat is either too little or too strong flavored, so additional duck, goose, pork, or a combination of these fats is used. The result is a succulent, tender, and surprisingly lean meat that is lightly salty and infused with seasonings. It may be eaten on its own simply roasted and crisped, or used as an ingredient in another dish, such as cassoulet or soup. Stored covered by the cooking fat, it has the potential to keep for over a year, ripening and becoming increasingly tender and velvety.

Apart from the savoriness of confit, it is also valuable for its convenience and economy. A store of confit in the refrigerator will supply you with quick and satisfying meals, many of which can be prepared in minutes. It is worth investing the time when you have it to make confit for the ease with which you can later prepare delicious, impromptu meals.

Most parts of the duck may be turned into confit. The breasts, however, are not as satisfying as the legs, which become very tender and silken while remaining moist. The legs of the Moulard or male Muscovy ducks are best prepared this way, as they are somewhat tough when roasted. As confit, the neck and wings will provide a light meal or snack, or can be used to season a soup. The hearts and gizzards become particularly tender and are delicious sliced and sautéed as part of a salad, used as an hors d'oeuvre, or put into a pâté.

Confit with Wine

The process of confit does wonders for the relationship between duck meat and red wines. With this method of curing, the musty gaminess of the meat is mellowed and the slight tang of astringency in the juices is eliminated. It is these factors that generally prevent a simple roasted duck from having a real affinity for a broad range of red wines. A sampling of confit with red wines, from the young and precocious to the rustic and hearty or well aged and refined, in a selection of varietals from around the world, demonstrates an incredible versatility. Of course, the meat does affect different wines in different ways. Generally, as do other meats, it will still tone down some of the harsh tannins in the wine and allow the fruit to show through. Some of the differences will lie in the character of the fruit and how it will blend with the herbal flavorings of the meat and the other components of the dish. Saltier versions of confit will tend to accentuate the wine's alcohol, an effect some people might find unpleasing on the palate.

Basic Method for Confit

This recipe has enough seasoning mix for about six duck legs with a few hearts, gizzards, and whole cloves of garlic tucked in. It is intended to give a basic understanding of the technique. The seasoning mix may be altered to suit your personal taste—more or less garlic, pepper, etc. Slow cooking is the key to a confit that is meltingly tender and almost falls away from the bone. The fat should barely simmer. If you have trouble regulating the heat on top of your stove, try using a heat diffuser or putting the confit in a low oven.

The finished confit may be eaten right away, but it is better to let it age in the fat for a while. Be sure there is at least an inch of fat covering the meat when you store it; otherwise it will spoil.

1   Combine the salt, pepper, garlic, shallots, cinnamon, cloves, bay leaves, and thyme, and mix thoroughly.

2   Place the duck legs in a glass or ceramic bowl and toss with the salt mixture. Cover and marinate in the refrigerator for 24 hours.

3   Remove the duck and rinse off the remaining marinade with cold water.

4   Melt the duck fat in a heavy-bottomed saucepan. There should be enough to cover the duck pieces. Place the duck in the fat, and over a medium flame, slowly bring the duck up to a very slight simmer.

4 tablespoons kosher salt

2 teaspoons ground pepper

4 cloves garlic, peeled and thinly sliced

2 large shallots, peeled and thinly sliced

1 cinnamon stick, crushed

2 whole cloves, crushed

4 bay leaves, crumbled

1 ½ teaspoons dry thyme

6 duck legs

6 cups rendered duck fat

5   How long the duck takes to cook will depend on the type, size, and part of the duck being used. Pekin duck legs may cook for only 1½–2 hours. Larger male Muscovy legs may take as long as 2½ hours. Wings, gizzards, and breasts may need only an hour.

To determine if the confit is ready, remove a piece from the fat and feel it. During the cooking process, the meat will get tight and tough and then relax. When it is done, it will feel soft and a small piece will pull away easily. Also, the tendon holding the meat to the ankle will separate and shrink back. Be careful not to cook it too much, or it will fall apart in the pot.

6   Gently remove the confit from the fat and place it in a ceramic or glass storage dish. Plastic will do if you are not storing it for too long. Let the fat cool to room temperature and pour it over the duck. There should be an inch of fat covering the duck with no meat poking through. Refrigerate. This will keep indefinitely.

See Confit with Wine discussion (page 122).

An American Southwestern Confit

This is a twist on the specialty of southwestern France using spices typical of American cuisine. The prickly pear compote is a nice tart foil for the meat. This recipe makes enough seasoning mix for about 6 duck legs.

Proceed according to the directions for the basic method (page 123).

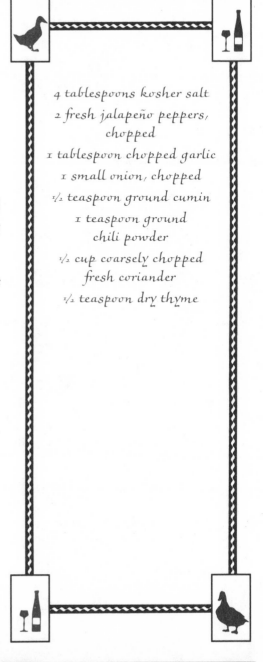

4 tablespoons kosher salt

2 fresh jalapeño peppers, chopped

1 tablespoon chopped garlic

1 small onion, chopped

½ teaspoon ground cumin

1 teaspoon ground chili powder

½ cup coarsely chopped fresh coriander

½ teaspoon dry thyme

Prickly Pear Compote

6 prickly pears
Juice of ½ lemon
Salt and pepper to taste

1   Peel the prickly pears and cut them into eight pieces each.

2   Pass them through a food mill to extract the pulp and remove the seeds.

3   Place the pulp in a small noncorrosive saucepan and cook over a medium-low flame until the pulp has thickened.

4   Season with the lemon juice, salt, and pepper. Chill before serving.

Roast Duck Confit with Braised Red Cabbage

Although we suggest using the legs, this recipe may be made with any part of duck confit you like.

1   Preheat the oven to 400°.

2   Heat the duck fat or olive oil in a 2-quart saucepan. Add the onion and sweat 1 minute.

3   Add the cabbage, apple, white wine, and duck stock. Mix well and cook slowly for ½ hour. Cover the saucepan and cook another ½ hour, or until the cabbage is soft. Season to taste with salt, pepper, and the vinegar.

4   While the cabbage is cooking, roast the duck confit for 20 minutes, then place it under the broiler just to crisp the skin. Serve with the cabbage.

The red cabbage in this dish is not so intensely flavored as sauerkraut, but it does introduce an element of acidity. This creates a situation that is not unlike the one mentioned in relation to the Confit with Apples, Onions, and Armagnac (page 128), and you will find that many of the same-style red wines show very well with this dish as well. If you prefer white wine, Riesling, and Gewürztraminer are interesting combinations, and a touch of sweetness can be very beneficial.

Confit with Apples, Onions, and Armagnac

SERVES 2

1 tablespoon duck fat or olive oil

1¼ cups duck confit, skin and bones removed, cut into bite-sized bits

1 cup apple (preferably Granny Smith), peeled and cut into ½-inch dice

¾ cup halved and thinly sliced onion

Pepper to taste

¼ cup Armagnac

This makes a fast meal that is appropriate for either lunch or dinner in any season. It is also a good way to use up odd pieces of confit. A green salad is all the accompaniment that is needed.

1   Heat a 10-inch skillet until very hot. Add the duck fat or olive oil. When it is just beginning to smoke, add the confit. Sauté 30 seconds, tossing occasionally.

2   Add the apple and onion to the skillet. Sauté 2–3 minutes, tossing occasionally until the apple is softened and everything is nicely browned.

3   Season to taste with pepper.

4   Remove the pan from the stove. Add the Armagnac all at once. Return the pan to the stove and stand back. *Be careful—the Armagnac will ignite.* When the flame dies out, toss and serve the confit.

This rustic, country-style dish actually has a very elegant balance of flavors. The confit has a seasoned saltiness that is complemented by the sweetness of the apples and charred onions. Saltiness always has a tendency to accent the alcohol in a wine, and combined with the acidity of the apples and onions, it is easy to upset the wonderful harmony that exists on the palate. For example, when the Armagnac flavor is combined with the food's salt and acidity, the accentuated alcohol often found in wines such as Crozes-Hermitage, Gigondas, or Zinfandel overtakes the wine's fruit and throws the wine out of balance. Red wines with a lush style of fruit, such as Cabernet Sauvignon, Merlot, or Shiraz from California or Australia, will be better suited. The charred onions have a mild sweetening effect on a wine's oaky flavors that is quite pleasant. Beyond taste, wines of a less-refined nature mirror the style and presentation of this dish.

Because it is so quick to prepare, the confit with apples, onions, and Armagnac is very appropriate for hotter weather. In such a context, this recipe can be beautifully matched with a variety of Riesling wines. Those on the drier side might be preferable, given the sweetening effect of the onions.

FATHER FINBARR O'BRIEN'S DUCK CONFIT SANDWICH

Originally ordained into the Holy Order of Egregious Saints in the County Mayo of Ireland, Father Finbarr O'Brien had an insatiable curiosity for many areas of art and science. The continual controversy created by his personal interests led to a conflict with his calling, and in his midlife Father Finbarr was finally defrocked. Released from the bonds of monastic life, he traveled to the European mainland and, on a walking pilgrimage, slowly made his way to Paris. He had no particular mission, except to see all the wondrous works of art and architecture that he had only read about and to witness firsthand the advancements and discoveries that were being made there. He was particularly intrigued by the way many of the great artists and philosophers of the time thought and spoke about the food they ate. After forty-odd years of boiled meat and potatoes, with only an occasional sip of poteen, he wondered whether it was such minds that inspired great food or if it was the food that inspired men to dream.

Traveling south from Paris, Finbarr, as he was now known, arrived in Gascony, where he had his first encounter with duck confit. So wondrous was this silky and savory delicacy that he decided to settle in the area for a time simply to learn the ritual that rendered such versatile meat. As the weather turned colder, his pack loaded with the cured duck meat, Finbarr ventured off in the direction of Italy.

It was the art and architecture of St. Peter's Basilica that drew him south through the culinary paradise of Provence and the wine and food regions of northern Italy. Arriving in Rome quite satiated physically, mentally, and spiritually, Finbarr began a study of art that would last the rest of his life.

Sadly enough, Father Finbarr O'Brien has not been immortalized for any substantial contribution to art or science. However, he did leave this world having made a very interesting culinary contribution, which, oddly enough, documents his trip from Mayo to Bologna. Never having forgotten the delicious variety of olives he tasted in Nice, or the sweet sun-dried tomatoes discovered in San Remo, he added to them a spicy hard salami, chewy Italian bread, and of course, a substantial layer of duck confit. His love of architecture is somewhat in evidence in the construction of this sandwich. Through his genius for spatial relations, the sandwich holds together quite perfectly throughout consumption and its contents never come spewing out the other end when bitten into.

The confit sandwich can be accompanied by a wide range of medium-bodied and quaffable red wines. Unfortunately, Finbarr never lived to see the development of the wine industry in the New World. California Zinfandel provides a special complement to this combination of flavors, particularly if chopped Kalamata olives are used in the sandwich.

A historical note:

The coined phrase "a religious experience," in its vulgar application to wine tasting and discussion, has been incorrectly attributed to Father Finbarr O'Brien.

Southwestern Duck Confit Burrito with Papaya Relish

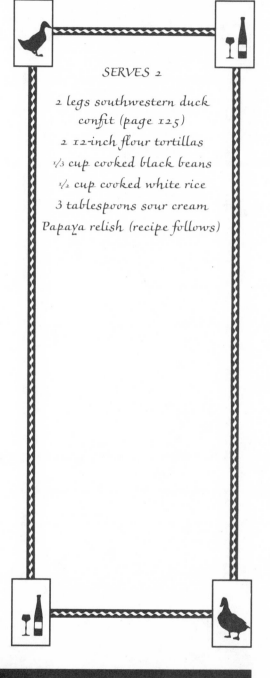

SERVES 2

2 legs southwestern duck
confit (page 125)
2 12-inch flour tortillas
1/3 cup cooked black beans
1/2 cup cooked white rice
3 tablespoons sour cream
Papaya relish (recipe follows)

Try substituting Prickly Pear Compote, page 126, for the papaya relish in this recipe.

1   Roast the duck confit in a 400° oven for 20 minutes to heat it through. Remove the skin and any fat from the legs.

2   Wrap the tortillas in foil and heat them in the oven for 7 minutes.

3   Remove the duck meat from the bones and roughly shred it, pulling it apart with two forks.

4   Heat the beans in a pan with some of their cooking liquid.

5   Lay the tortillas out flat. Divide the shredded duck meat, beans, rice, sour cream, and papaya relish between them.

6   Roll up the tortillas, folding in the ends as you go. Serve with hot sauce if you wish.

Papaya Relish

1 papaya, peeled and cut in
¼-inch dice
jalapeño pepper, seeded and
finely diced
1 small red onion, peeled and
finely diced
Juice of 1 lime
½ teaspoon kosher salt

1   Mix all ingredients and let stand at room temperature for at least one hour.

Cassoulet, the traditional dish of Gascony, is a bean and confit combination whose ingredients are similar to those in this recipe. You will find that the wines of Cahors and Madiran show the same affinity for the burrito that they do for the beans and confit of the cassoulet. Keeping with an American theme, a fruitier-styled Zinfandel would give the same effect.

Full- and fat-styled Chardonnays from California and Australia, if hearty enough, will echo the fruit of the papaya.

Choucroute with Confit and Duck Sausage

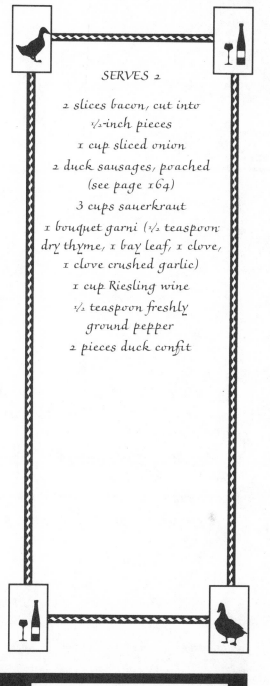

SERVES 2

2 slices bacon, cut into
½-inch pieces
1 cup sliced onion
2 duck sausages, poached
(see page 164)
3 cups sauerkraut
1 bouquet garni (½ teaspoon
dry thyme, 1 bay leaf, 1 clove,
1 clove crushed garlic)
1 cup Riesling wine
½ teaspoon freshly
ground pepper
2 pieces duck confit

This is a simple variation on the classic Alsatian dish. You can vary the meats as you like, using regular roasted duck, gizzards, smoked duck, and even duck livers. Directions are given here for preparing it in a sauté pan that can be put in the oven, but any shallow casserole will do, as long as it can be used both on a flame and in the oven. Alternatively, you can cook the bacon and onions in a sauté pan and then transfer them to a casserole and finish assembling the dish.

1   Sauté the bacon until crisp in a 10-inch frying pan. Remove with a slotted spoon and reserve. Pour off all but 1 tablespoon of the bacon fat (or if there is less than that amount, make up the difference with olive oil).

2   Add the onion and sausages and sauté about 5 minutes over medium heat, until the onion is translucent and everything is slightly browned.

3   Return the bacon to the pan along with the sauerkraut, the bouquet garni, wine, and pepper. Stir to combine.

4   Nestle the duck confit in the sauerkraut. Cover and place in a 350° oven for about 1 hour, until everything is hot and juicy.

5   To serve, remove the bouquet garni. Place the sauerkraut on a serving platter and arrange the meats around it. Pour the juices over all.

The herbal silkiness of the confit and the garlic and pepper of the duck sausage are secondary to the dominant flavors of the sauerkraut, which imparts a succulent pickled flavor to the confit. The most influential element of the sauerkraut, however, is its acidity, which will render most wines utterly flavorless. A wine with a touch of sweetness to balance this acidity will complement the dish very well. Beer is much more appropriate, both as a flavor combination and to suit the ambiance the dish is likely to create.

THE DUCK PRESS

In Paris, along the Seine, stands one of France's most exclusive restaurants, Tour D'Argent, which is famous for its view of Notre Dame and also quite renowned for its pressed duck. The dinner is presented with great fanfare and spectacle, and upon the completion of your meal, you will actually receive a postcard stating the serial number of the duck you just ate. Possibly one of the best-kept secrets in the French restaurant industry is that pressed duck is a rather simple means of preparation, and if you like, it can be quite a lot of fun.

Dining together is a universal bonding ritual that can be heightened by sharing the preparation of the meal. As a conversation piece, the duck press is the sort of gadget that tends to involve people who are not normally interested in cooking. All members of the party will want to try their hand at turning the press and rendering the juices. Think of it as the French version of the Great American Barbeque, where people stand about the chef, watching and kibitzing, and are inspired to actively participate.

The downside of this ritual is that a solid brass duck press is likely to cost several hundred dollars, and its use is generally limited to special occasions. It is, however, a lovely objet d'art for any kitchen or dining room and is durable enough to be passed around to family and friends for generations to come.

Pressed Duck

Also known as duck Rouennais, pressed duck is a classic French specialty often made with Rouen ducks. Traditionally it included the technique of smothering rather than bleeding the duck, which produced a richer meat. It is the carcass, not the meat, that is pressed to extract the juices that will thicken your sauce and enrich it with light, livery flavors. The same results can be obtained without a duck press by chopping the carcass and passing it through a meat grinder. The resulting mixture must then be strained through a very fine sieve.

Here we present a modern version of the original classic. The breast is sautéed separately, rather than roasted on the bone, fileted, then reheated in the sauce. Be sure to use a good quality, full-bodied wine for your sauce.

1 Preheat the oven to 350°.

2 Remove the duck breasts from the carcass and render the fat from the skin according to the directions on page 21.

3 Leave the legs on the carcass, sprinkle the whole with salt and pepper, and roast for 20 minutes. Remove the legs from the carcass and return them to the roasting pan, cooking them another 25 minutes, or until crisp and done. Reserve the carcasses.

4 While the legs are roasting, prepare the sauce. Sweat the shallots in the duck fat or olive oil for 5 minutes. Add the red wine and reduce about 5 minutes, to ¼ cup.

5 Add the stock and thyme and bring to a boil. Reduce about 10 minutes, to about ⅔ cup. The sauce should be a little thin at this point as it will be thickened with the duck juices. Remove and discard the thyme sprigs.

SERVES 4–6

2 5-pound Pekin, Muscovy, or Rouen ducks

Kosher salt and pepper to taste

1 small shallot, finely chopped

1½ teaspoons duck fat or olive oil

¾ cup red wine

1½ cups duck stock

2 sprigs fresh thyme

6 While the sauce is reducing, press the duck carcasses. Chop them up with a cleaver into 3 or 4 pieces each and place them in your duck press. Place a bowl under the spout and turn the handle as much as possible. Press the carcasses until ½ cup of juice is rendered, then unscrew the press and discard the remains.

7 When ready to serve, sauté the breasts to the desired doneness (see page 20). Bring the sauce to a boil, lower it to below a simmer, and whisk in the pressed duck juices. Do not boil the sauce after you have done this or it will curdle. Gently heat it through until hot.

8 Slice the duck breasts lengthwise into five or six pieces each. Place some sauce on two plates, place a duck leg on top of it, and arrange the breast slices in a fanned presentation. Serve the extra sauce on the side.

This is delicious accompanied by a creamy gratin or some buttered egg noodles.

The intensified duck flavor of this dish decreases the meat's affinity for most lighter red wines. Another complication is that carcasses will yield varying degrees of liver flavor. Full-bodied Pinot Noir will be as glorious as ever, and wines based on the Sangiovese Grosso grape have the assertive, dry fruit and flavor to stand next to this sauce. A wonderful revelation occurs when paring this dish with a Barolo or Barbaresco. These Nebbiolo-based wines normally overpower most foods, including the pleasant gaminess of plain duck meat. However, their combination with pressed duck creates a big, heady and gamy meat experience.

DUCK IN CHINESE TRADITION

The Chinese are great lovers of duck, and wisely devote the fourth day of the new year to its celebration. They take the duck for all it's worth, enjoying its various parts in many dishes. One cannot walk through a Chinatown anywhere in the United States without seeing gorgeous roast ducks, head and feet intact, hanging in shop and restaurant windows. A closer look will reveal duck in many forms—pressed and dried, salted and made into "hams," salted eggs to be used as a seasoning, sweetish duck liver sausages, duck feet, and the famous thousand-year-old egg.

China has given us not only the Pekin, which was first bred there over a thousand years ago, but the Pekin in its most sublime form—the Peking Duck (see below). Chinese duck is also prepared braised, possibly with black mushrooms; as a whole boned and stuffed crispy duck; stir-fried; or combined with other ingredients in a salad. Such Chinese innovations might include a salad with shreds of duck, skin intact, tossed with tender shreds of chicken, long cool strips of jellyfish, and pickled vegetables. Chinese folklore has it that duck soup is so healthful and beneficial that it can reconcile estranged husbands and wives.

Chinese cuisine is appreciative of texture as well as taste, and this appreciation allows the Chinese to be creative with parts of the duck, such as the tongue and feet, that others might throw away. The skin of the feet has great texture—firm and slightly chewy, yet tender—and it absorbs the flavors of whatever it is cooked with. Duck feet dishes are a peasant specialty of the southern regions. Although these preparations are now becoming less common, as they are considered old-fashioned and unsophisticated, the trouble is still sometimes taken to bone the feet whole, a complicated and time-consuming task. It is more fun, however, to eat the foot with the bone in and to perfect one's method. It is quite impressive to watch a veteran duck-foot-eater put the entire webbed foot in his mouth and munch away, spitting out a little bone from time to time and working the whole thing clean without using his fingers at all.

Peking Duck

SERVES 2–4

1 5-pound Pekin duck
1 bunch scallions, whites and
tops separated
4 ½-inch slices ginger
¼ cup honey
¾ cup hoisin sauce
1 tablespoon sesame oil
1 teaspoon Madeira
(optional)

For those who honor the duck, this specialty from northern China is the best way to glorify its being. The care taken in this preparation brings the duck skin to sublime perfection, leaving the meat tender, succulent, and seemingly fatless. It is often served as part of a great banquet, and is traditionally presented in three courses: the crackling skin wrapped in pancakes with scallion and hoisin or bean sauce, the meat stir-fried with vegetables, and the carcass made into soup, exemplifying the duck's economy and versatility. Here, however, we present it as a single, elaborate course, to be enjoyed all at once.

1   Remove any excess fat from the duck cavity and reserve it for another use. Rinse the duck and pat dry.

2   Using butcher's twine, tie the duck tightly around the loose neck skin or slip the twine under the wings to hang the duck suspended in a breezy spot (not in direct sunshine) for 3½ hours. Place a pan underneath to catch the drippings.

3   Bring 2 gallons of water to a boil in a large pot with the scallion tops, the ginger, and the honey.

4   Holding the duck by the string, lower it into the boiling water, turning it to scald all sides, for 30 seconds. Remove and rehang the duck, leaving it to dry for 3 hours.

5   Make scallion brushes by using a small, sharp knife to cut lengthwise slits in either end of the white parts of the scallion. Be careful to leave a section in the middle uncut. Soak the scallions in ice water so the ends will curl up.

6 Place the duck on the counter. Being careful not to break the skin at any point, start at the cavity end and slowly and gently separate the skin from the meat, using your fingers and a small knife. Continue until you are halfway through the duck, including the skin around the legs. Then turn the duck around to repeat the procedure from the neck end. Be careful not to stretch the skin or it will crack. Do not worry about separating the skin on the wings.

7 Using a trussing needle and butcher's twine, close the cavity of the duck. Trim the neck skin to about two inches and tie it tightly closed.

8 Using a basketball pump, carefully inflate the skin by inserting the pin into the neck opening, squeezing it through where you have tied it closed. Be sure the pin is between the skin and the meat. Inflate the duck until it is taut, but be careful not to overinflate it or the skin will crack. (If you do not have a pump, you may omit this step and still get excellent results.)

9 Carefully place the duck breast side up on a rack set in a roasting pan and cook in a 350° oven for 40 minutes.

10 Lower the temperature to 300°, gently turn the duck over, and roast another 30 minutes. Turn the duck breast side up again, and roast another 30 minutes, until the skin is golden brown.

11 Remove the duck from the oven and let it rest for five minutes.

12 While the duck is resting, prepare the sauce by combining the hoisin, sesame oil, and Madeira.

13 *To serve:* Remove the legs and place them on either end of a large platter. With a sharp knife, remove the breast skin, slicing along the breastbone. It will come away quite easily. Place the skin on a cutting board and cut it into pieces about 1 inch x 2 inches. Remove the breast filets and cut them into 1-inch-wide slices. Arrange the breast meat in the center of the platter, with the skin around it. Garnish the platter with the scallion brushes. Serve with the hoisin sauce and hot Mandarin Pancakes (see page 170).

The flavors found in Peking duck suggest the accompaniment of a big, well-fruited wine. Riesling, with its stronger flavor and apple-like fruit, is probably the best solution. However, rather than matching intensity with intensity, it can also be interesting simply to try a wine that has a good acidity and a crisp, austere style of fruit that whets the palate without adding to the already complex flavors. A nice Bourgogne Blanc, Chablis, or other Chardonnay without too much oakiness will provide such a subdued accompaniment.

Casserole of Braised Duck Feet with Black Mushrooms

SERVES 12

12 duck feet
1 cup vegetable or soy oil
2 cups water
1/4 cup dark soy sauce
1 scallion, sliced
5 1/4-inch slices ginger
1/2 teaspoon kosher salt
1/3 cup sherry or Chinese rice wine
1 teaspoon sugar
2 pieces of star anise
10 dried shiitake mushrooms
3 cups roughly torn romaine lettuce or Chinese cabbage leaves
2 teaspoons cornstarch, combined with just enough cold water to dissolve it

This recipe was given to us by Mrs. Nora Chu, who, together with her husband Kelvin, owns the wonderful Phoenix Garden restaurant in New York City's Chinatown, which is known for contemporary as well as classic Cantonese cuisine.

1   Trim the duck feet of any nails. Blanch them in boiling water for 1 minute. Drain and pat dry.

2   Heat the vegetable or soy oil to about 400°. Fry the duck feet for about three minutes, until they are lightly browned. Be careful, as they will splatter.

3   In a 3½-quart saucepan, combine the water, soy sauce, scallion, ginger, salt, sherry or rice wine, sugar, and star anise. Add the duck feet and bring to a simmer. Simmer for about 1 hour, until the duck feet are tender. Remove the duck feet and strain the liquid, reserving 1½ cups and discarding the rest.

4 Soak the mushrooms in warm water for 20 minutes until softened. Remove them from the water and discard the liquid. Steam the mushrooms for 1 hour over a little of the liquid in which the duck feet are cooking. Return this steaming liquid to the pot with the duck feet.

5 Place the lettuce in the bottom of a stove-top casserole. Arrange the duck feet on top, then the mushrooms, and pour the strained cooking liquid over all. Bring the casserole to a rapid boil, lower the heat, and add the cornstarch. Heat until just thickened, about 30 seconds, and serve.

Wine and duck feet will prove to be a battle of textures rather than a combining of flavors. A rich sparkling wine will provide the needed palate-cleansing accompaniment.

Breast of Moulard Braised in Riesling with Glazed Endive

1 Remove the skin from the Moulard breast and reserve it for another use.

2 In a 10-inch skillet, heat the duck fat or olive oil over a high flame. When it just begins to smoke, add the duck breast and quickly brown it on both sides.

3 Remove the breast and wipe out any excess fat from the pan. Deglaze with the Riesling.

4 Add the stock and bring to a boil. Lower the heat to a simmer and add the duck breast and a pinch of salt. Braise the duck breast slowly for about 12 minutes, turning it once, until medium rare. Remove the duck breast from the pan and let it rest in a warm spot while you finish the sauce.

5 Raise the heat to high and add the butter. Reduce until a saucelike consistency is achieved. Season with salt and pepper.

6 Holding your knife at a 45° angle to the cutting board, slice the duck breast crosswise into about 8 pieces. Divide the sauce between two warmed plates and arrange the meat on top. Garnish with the glazed endive.

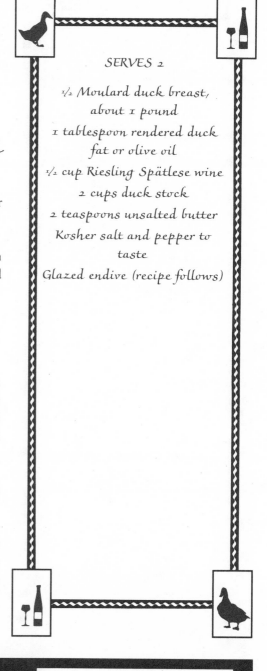

SERVES 2

½ Moulard duck breast, about 1 pound

1 tablespoon rendered duck fat or olive oil

½ cup Riesling Spätlese wine

2 cups duck stock

2 teaspoons unsalted butter

Kosher salt and pepper to taste

Glazed endive (recipe follows)

Glazed Endive

1 large endive
1 tablespoon olive oil
1/2 teaspoon sugar
Pinch of salt

1 Cut the endive in quarters lengthwise. Remove the core and cut each quarter in half lengthwise.

2 Heat the olive oil in an 8-inch skillet over medium heat. Add the endive and sauté, tossing occasionally, for about 5 minutes.

3 Sprinkle with the sugar and salt and continue cooking for another 5 minutes, or until the endive is soft and browned.

A distinctive feature of most dry or sweet Rieslings is a nice, tart, fruitiness reminiscent of apples. In fact, you will find that the quality of this finished sauce is more apple-like in character than that of the Apple Cider Sauce (page 41). While this flavor is well suited to the intensity of the meat, the fruit of red wines that might normally be paired with magret will simply fall short. Serving the same Riesling used in the sauce works well, but does not provide the intrigue of an additional flavor dimension. A well-made Chardonnay with a crisp, lean style of fruit would show a more interesting flavor variety with this dish.

Crispy Moulard Cutlets with Walnut Sauce

The advantages of turning Moulard into cutlets is threefold. Not only does it serve to tenderize, but it extends the value of this rather expensive but worthy duck meat. Most significantly, the cutlets allow for a more thorough penetration of the marinade, which will complement and utilize the intensity of the Moulard's distinct character. It is important not to slice the meat too thin in order to retain its flavor and texture.

Since it is difficult to make the small amount of walnut sauce necessary for this recipe, we have given measurements for a larger quantity than is actually needed. The sauce is also delicious served with chicken or tossed with hot pasta, and it keeps indefinitely in the refrigerator.

1   Holding your knife at about a 30-degree angle to the cutting board and slicing the meat against the grain, cut the breast into ½-inch slices. Gently smack each slice with the flat side of your knife to even it, but be careful not to tear the meat. Marinate the slices in the wine for 2 hours.

2   Lightly dredge each slice in flour, then egg, then bread-crumbs. Lay them flat on a plate, so that they are not touching, while you make the sauce.

3   Combine all the ingredients for the sauce in a blender or food processor. Process until emulsified, but make sure to leave it a little chunky.

SERVES 2

½ Moulard breast, about 1 pound, skin removed and reserved for another use
½ cup Riesling wine
Flour for dredging
1 egg, beaten with a little water
Breadcrumbs for dredging
¼ cup vegetable oil for frying
Kosher salt to taste
1 tablespoon chopped parsley for garnish

FOR THE SAUCE
1 cup walnuts
1 anchovy
1 clove garlic, peeled
2 tablespoons freshly grated Parmesan cheese
Juice of ½ lemon
Kosher salt and pepper to taste
¾ cup olive oil

4   Heat the vegetable oil in a 10-inch skillet. Add the breaded duck slices, sprinkle with salt, and quickly fry them until browned, turning once. Arrange the duck on two warmed plates and top with some of the sauce. Sprinkle with the chopped parsley.

This is nice served with steamed green beans and some barley cooked in a little duck fat with onions.

This recipe uses a marinade of Riesling wine, but there are endless alternatives to experiment with. Gaminess is complemented with other flavors, increasing its capacity for unusual wine combinations. For instance, these cutlets will still taste good with a Pinot Noir, but they are also delicious with a full-bodied dry or off-dry Riesling. Dry rosé will also complement the meat and is particularly nice with the walnut sauce.

Fricassee of Duck with Mushrooms and Polenta

Because of the nature of this dish, it is difficult to remove the rendered fat. It is therefore best to use a breed of duck that has a lower fat content. This moist cooking method is also well suited to cooking wild duck, which is leaner and tougher.

1   Remove the wings at the second joint and reserve them for another use. Quarter the duck.

2   Over a medium flame, heat the duck fat or olive oil in a 10-inch skillet with straight sides. Dredge the duck in the flour and add to the skillet, browning it on all sides. Remove and reserve.

3   Add the mushrooms and garlic to the skillet and brown, stirring occasionally, for 5 minutes.

4   Return the duck to the pan and add the white wine. Bring to a boil and reduce the liquid by half.

5   Add 1 cup of duck stock, bring to a boil, and lower to a simmer. Simmer for 45 minutes.

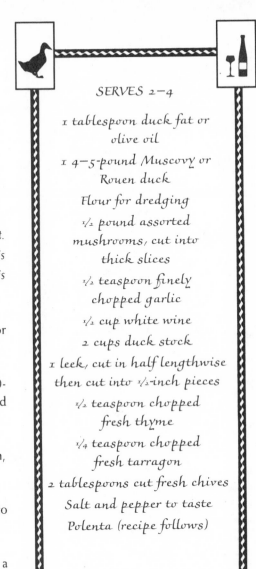

SERVES 2–4

1 tablespoon duck fat or olive oil

1 4–5-pound Muscovy or Rouen duck

Flour for dredging

1/2 pound assorted mushrooms, cut into thick slices

1/2 teaspoon finely chopped garlic

1/2 cup white wine

2 cups duck stock

1 leek, cut in half lengthwise then cut into 1/2-inch pieces

1/2 teaspoon chopped fresh thyme

1/4 teaspoon chopped fresh tarragon

2 tablespoons cut fresh chives

Salt and pepper to taste

Polenta (recipe follows)

6   Add the leek and continue simmering for another 35 minutes, or until the duck is tender. Skim the fat occasionally. You may have to add more stock if it evaporates too quickly. Keep the level about halfway up the pieces of duck.

7   Add the chopped herbs, salt, and pepper and simmer another 10 minutes.

8   Remove the duck to a warmed platter. Let the contents of the pan stand a few minutes and skim any fat that comes to the surface. Pour the mushroom mixture over the duck. Serve with polenta.

Polenta

1. Combine the stock, milk, salt, pepper, and the 1 teaspoon duck fat in a heavy 3-quart saucepan. Bring to a boil.

2. Place the cornmeal in a strainer or sifter and slowly sift it into the boiling liquid, whisking continually.

3. Over low heat, continue whisking the polenta until it thickens and no longer tastes raw, about 5 minutes. Make sure you are scraping the bottom of the pot with the whisk so that the polenta does not stick.

4. Scrape the polenta into a 9- x 9-inch baking pan that has been greased with duck fat. Smooth the top with a wet spatula. Let set until firm, about half an hour. Refrigerate if not using immediately.

5. Cut the polenta into shapes such as squares or circles. You can either sauté them in a hot pan or heat them in the oven on a greased baking sheet until browned.

This fricassee is strictly red wine fare. Both the flavor and the robustness of Rhône wines such as Gigondas or Châteauneuf-du-Pape make a nice accompaniment to this rustic dish. A peppery Zinfandel also adds an interesting dimension.

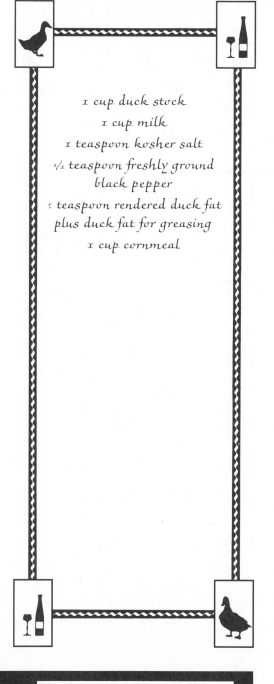

1 cup duck stock

1 cup milk

1 teaspoon kosher salt

1/2 teaspoon freshly ground black pepper

1 teaspoon rendered duck fat plus duck fat for greasing

1 cup cornmeal

Sautéed Red Snapper with Foie Gras Sauce

SERVES 2

2 8-ounce filets of red snapper, skin intact

Kosher salt and pepper to taste

1 tablespoon rendered duck fat

½ cup rosé champagne*

3 tablespoons duck demi-glace

1½ ounces pureed, cooked foie gras

This is a fine way to utilize the end of a whole-liver foie gras terrine, which may not be attractive enough to serve by itself.

1   With a sharp knife, lightly score the skin side of the snapper in a cross-hatched pattern. Season with salt and pepper.

2   In a 10-inch skillet, heat the duck fat over high heat until it just begins to smoke. Add the snapper, skin side down, and sauté until the skin is golden and crispy, about 2 minutes. Turn the filets over and cook another 30 seconds to 1 minute, depending on the thickness of the fish. Remove to two warmed plates.

3   Wipe the pan clean of any excess fat and deglaze with the champagne. Reduce by half.

4   Add the demi-glace and reduce by half.

5   Turn off the flame and whisk in the foie gras, a little at a time, to thicken the sauce. Season with salt and pepper.

6   Pour the sauce around the filets and serve.

---

* If not serving rosé champagne with this dish, you may use another full-bodied white wine for the sauce.

Roast potatoes, turnips, and sautéed mushrooms make a nice accompaniment.

Foie gras sauce has a rich flavor that garnishes the fish very nicely, yet its consistency is much lighter than one might expect. The flavor of the snapper offers a nice backdrop for many different types of full-bodied white wines and a selection of reds as well. Sparkling wine will be most elegant—don't hesitate to serve up your finest rosé champagne for extra richness and an added dimension of color coordination. Puligny-Montrachet or a similar-styled Chardonnay would be a wonderful second choice. Pinot Noir also gets a rave review with this dish, so long as you choose a wine in a lighter, more fragrant style that is not too excessively barrel-fermented.

Tongue and Cheek

SERVES 2

6 duck tongues

1/3 cup white wine

1 small shallot,
finely chopped

1 cup fish stock

3/4 pound cod cheeks*

Large pinch saffron

1 bunch spinach, washed

2 tablespoons unsalted butter

1/2 small carrot, julienned

1 large leek, white part
only, julienned

1 tablespoon peeled and
seeded tomato cut in
medium dice

Kosher salt and pepper
to taste

2 tablespoons chives, cut in
1/2-inch pieces

Squeeze of lemon

It is said that this recipe was developed in the Mekong Delta by a Vietnamese chef of partly French descent who was concerned about his unattached, extremely shy daughter. After he served it to her on her sixteenth birthday, she became, to his amazement, outgoing, delightfully precocious, and before long, the most popular young woman in the village. Carefully guarding his secret, the chef began to market his dish to the local gentry and political rulers and amassed great wealth. Today his descendants reside in the Adams Morgan section of Washington, D.C., and do a very brisk business, particularly during election years or when Congress is in session.

1   Cook the tongues in boiling water for 10 minutes. Drain. When cool enough to handle, pull out the bone from the center and the cartilage running down the bottom. Cut each tongue into about eight pieces.

2   In a 10-inch sauté pan, combine the wine and shallot. Bring to a boil and reduce by half.

3   Add the stock, bring to a boil, and lower to a simmer. Add the cod cheeks and the saffron and poach gently until almost done, about 2–3 minutes. Remove to a plate and keep warm. Reserve the liquid in the pan.

4   Steam the spinach, using only the water clinging to the leaves, until wilted. Arrange in a ring on two warmed plates and keep warm.

* Substitute filet of cod or sole if cod cheeks are unavailable.

5 Bring the liquid to a boil again and add the butter, carrot, and leek. Reduce until the butter is emulsified and the sauce has a light, silky, still brothlike consistency. Add the tomato, salt, pepper, chives, lemon, and duck tongues. Heat through.

6 Place the cod cheeks in the center of the spinach and top with the sauce.

Served either as an appetizer or entrée, this easy preparation presents a rather stunning display of color. Tongue and cheek is as subtle in flavor as it is vibrantly colored by the saffron, leeks, spinach, and carrots. It's a white wine dish calling for very crisp and clean fruit without any oak. Many of the affordable white wines of Spain, Italy, or southern France will provide the austere accompaniment that permits the delicate fish and saffron flavors to show through.

Grilled Duck Breast with Duck Fat Béarnaise

SERVES 2 GASCONS
OR 4 AMERICANS

½ cup white wine

¼ cup tarragon vinegar

2 tablespoons finely
chopped shallots

2 tablespoons finely chopped
fresh tarragon

2 egg yolks

½–¾-cup rendered duck fat

Salt and pepper to taste

½ Moulard duck breast

This recipe comes from David Waltuck of Chanterelle restaurant in New York City. He suggests serving it with some potatoes fried in duck fat with wild mushrooms and garlic and a seasonal green vegetable.

1   In a 1½-quart noncorrosive saucepan, combine the white wine, vinegar, shallots, and 1 tablespoon tarragon. Bring to a boil and reduce to about 2 tablespoons.

2   Place the egg yolks in a stainless steel bowl. Add the reduction to the yolks, whisking well while you pour.

3   Place the bowl over a pot of simmering water. The water should not touch the bottom of the bowl. Whisk the egg mixture continually until it becomes fluffy, thick, and hot, about 1–2 minutes. Be careful not to let the eggs get too hot or they will curdle. Remove from the heat and set aside.

4   While you are whisking, heat the duck fat to the same temperature as the egg yolk mixture. Slowly add the duck fat to the egg yolks, whisking it in a spoonful at a time. If the béarnaise gets too thick, thin it out with a little warm water.

5   Add the remaining tablespoon of tarragon and season with salt and pepper. You can keep the sauce warm by covering it with plastic wrap and placing it in a warm spot until needed.

6   Remove the skin from the duck breast and reserve it for another use. Grill the breast over a high flame until the outside is well browned and the inside is still rare. Let it rest for a minute and then slice it thinly crosswise and fan it onto two warmed plates. Nap with the béarnaise sauce and serve.

Eggs often make it difficult to achieve a good food and wine match, but this béarnaise sauce has plenty of other ingredients countering their influence. There is a wonderful sharpness resulting from the shallot, vinegar, and white wine reduction, and these elements combine to create a pronounced acidity that counters the effect the egg yolk might have on certain wines. The sauce is a rich complement to the flavor of duck but won't assist wines such as Cabernet or Merlot, which don't normally blend well with its gaminess. This richness, rather, requires acidity in a wine, and fuller Pinot Noir blends particularly well with the hints of tarragon.

BARBEQUE AND SAUSAGE

Barbequed Duck

Achieving a barbequed duck with fat rendered and a skin that is nicely charred and crisp but not burnt is possible, but it takes a bit of fiddling. One technique is to roast the duck parts for about 20 minutes in a 350° oven to render the fat, and then to finish cooking the duck on a hot grill. Another technique is to move the coals to either side, place a pan of water directly beneath the grilling duck, and close the barbeque lid. This will keep the dripping fat from flaring up and burning the duck. It also slows down the cooking, allowing more time for the fat to render. You can move the duck to a hotter part of the grill for a final browning. Either way, the cooking will take about 30–45 minutes, depending on the hotness of your fire, wind conditions, and the degree of doneness desired.

Each and every American has his or her own special routine when it comes to barbeque. Cooking-out somehow gets deeply rooted in traditions that just aren't to be interfered with. That one should actually sit and pontificate on a series of rigid guidelines for which wine will best accompany which marinade is likely to place a damper on any backyard gathering. *But* here, most tactfully, are a few suggestions for those who might want to drink wine with their barbequed

duck. If serving white wine, find a full-styled one with good fruit that will counter the spices. A Chardonnay with well-pronounced barrel fermentation is particularly nice with the Barbequed Duck with Pineapple and Plantains (page 164). Lighter-styled Pinot Noir works well in the summer, and can be moderately chilled. Zinfandel is a good accompaniment for all grilled foods and particularly nice with the charred spicy sweetness of the Traditional Barbeque Sauce (page 161). Fruity whites will work better than reds with the chili-rubbed barbequed duck (page 160). The most crucial characteristic for any wine to be served with barbeque is a crisp and firm palate-cleansing acidity.

Honey-Soy Barbequed Duck

1 In a 1½-quart saucepan, simmer all the ingredients for 5 minutes. Let cool.

2 The easiest way to marinate the duck is to place the pieces in a resealable plastic storage bag with the marinade. This will keep all areas of the duck in contact with the marinade and eliminate the need for turning the duck over occasionally.

3 Marinate 24 hours, refrigerated.

4 Remove from the marinade and barbeque according to one of the methods on page 157. Baste with the marinade from time to time.

MAKES ENOUGH
SAUCE FOR ONE
QUARTERED DUCK, TO
SERVE 2–4

3 tablespoons clover honey
½ cup soy sauce
4 ¼-inch slices fresh ginger
1 scallion, sliced
1 teaspoon hot sauce

Chili-Rubbed Barbequed Duck

MAKES ENOUGH MARINADE FOR ONE QUARTERED DUCK, TO SERVE 2–4

1 small onion
Juice of 6 limes
8 teaspoons chili powder
2 tablespoons olive oil

1   Peel the onion and cut it into small pieces. Place in a blender and pulverize.

2   Combine the onion with the rest of the ingredients. Rub all over the duck and marinate, refrigerated, 24 hours.

3   Remove the duck from the marinade and barbeque according to one of the methods on page 157.

Traditional Barbeque Sauce

1   Heat the olive oil in a 2-quart saucepan. Add the garlic and onion, and over medium-low heat, cook, stirring occasionally, until they are translucent.

2   Add the rest of the ingredients and simmer for 15 minutes.

Note: Begin basting the duck with this sauce about halfway through cooking, when much of the fat has been rendered and the duck is beginning to brown.

MAKES ENOUGH
FOR ONE
QUARTERED DUCK, TO
SERVE 2–4

1 tablespoon olive oil
1 tablespoon finely
chopped garlic
1 onion, minced
2 cups ketchup
2 teaspoons Worcestershire
sauce
2 tablespoons red
wine vinegar
1 teaspoon Dijon mustard
1 tablespoon chili powder
1/4 teaspoon ground
black pepper
1 tablespoon hot sauce
Juice of 1 lemon
2 tablespoons butter
1 teaspoon dark brown sugar

Barbequed Duck with Pineapple and Plantains

SERVES 4–20

2 Pekin ducks, quartered, with boneless breasts

2 cups pineapple juice

1 cup pineapple preserves

1/4 cup honey

Salt and pepper to taste

1 pineapple, cut into quarters and trimmed

2 sweet plantains, peeled and sliced 1/2-inch thick

Olive oil for brushing

This can easily be translated into quantities big enough to feed a large party. For a more festive presentation, especially when there is a lot of other food at an informal gathering, the duck, pineapple, and plantains can be barbequed and then cut into bite-size pieces and skewered, eliminating the need for plates and silverware and providing for easy cleanup.

1   Roast the duck legs in a 350° oven for 20 minutes to render some of the fat. Render the fat from the breasts according to the directions for how to cook a duck breast on page 21, cooking the skin side only.

2   Combine the pineapple juice, preserves, and honey in a bowl and mix thoroughly.

3   Grill the duck over a medium-hot fire, basting it with the pineapple juice mixture and seasoning it with the salt and pepper. Turn it frequently to brown evenly. How long it will take to cook depends on your fire, wind conditions, and the degree of doneness desired. You can estimate 10 minutes for medium-cooked breasts and 20–30 minutes for well-done legs.

4   Brush the pineapple and plantains with olive oil and season them with salt and pepper. Grill next to the duck, for about 5 minutes, turning so that they brown on all sides.

5   Slice the pineapple and serve it with the duck and plantains, or cut everything up into bite-size pieces and skewer, as described above.

Spicy Duck Sausage

MAKES APPROXIMATELY 16 4-INCH SAUSAGES

3 pounds uncooked duck meat

1½ pounds pork fat back

1 cup red wine

1 medium Spanish onion, sliced

10 cloves garlic, crushed

5 bay leaves

1 tablespoon kosher salt

1 teaspoon coarsely ground black pepper

1 teaspoon ground white pepper

1 teaspoon spicy red pepper flakes

½ teaspoon ground clove

1 teaspoon dry thyme

Large pinch ground nutmeg

5–6 feet hog casing, soaked and rinsed

It is best to make these zesty sausages with meat taken from the legs. Breast meat will work just as well, although it seems a shame to grind up such beautiful meat. An ideal way to cook the sausages is on an outdoor barbeque, which gives them a charred smokiness that enhances the gaminess of the duck and spices. You may also cook them as you would confit or sauté them with excellent results. They are delicious served with many garnishes, including braised cabbage, apple or Prickly Pear Compote (page 126), Papaya Relish (page 132), fried onions, Polenta (page 149), or in a choucroute (see page 133).

1   Cut the duck meat and fat back into pieces that will fit through your meat grinder. Combine them with the red wine, onion, garlic, and bay leaves. Cover and marinate overnight in the refrigerator.

2   Remove and discard the bay leaves. Drain the wine from the sausage mix. Fit your grinder with the coarse grinding plate and pass everything through twice.

3   Add all the seasonings to the ground meat and mix very thoroughly.

4   To fill the casings, you can use either the sausage stuffer attachment to your grinder or a large pastry bag fitted with a straight tip. For the latter method, fill the bag with the sausage mix. Cut the hog casing into two-foot lengths. Tie a knot in one end of the casing and gather it all onto the tip of the pastry bag.

With one hand around the tip to guide the sausage as it is filled, squeeze the bag with your other hand. The casing should be full, but not stuffed too tightly, as it will expand when cooked. Tie another knot to close the casing. Use butcher's twine to tie off links about 4–5 inches long. Repeat with the remaining casing until all the filling is used up.

5   Place the sausage in a large pot and cover with cold water. Place on the stove and heat to just below the boiling point. If the sausages are firm at this point, remove them from the water and cool. If they aren't, let them cool in the water. They are now ready for grilling or sautéing.

Duck sausage is another item that offers cross-seasonal appeal, but these are extraspecial served hot off the grill. Many red wines will show adequately, but none seems to be so well suited as the character of the Zinfandel grape to match the charred flavors of the meat seasoned with sweet thyme, red pepper flakes, and garlic. Because of the popular blush wine that is usually made from these grapes, the varietal is somewhat misunderstood in today's market. The full red is produced in a wide range of styles, some light enough to provide excellent summertime drinking. Check the label and be aware that many Zinfandels have an alcohol level approaching 14 percent, which may affect your personal preference in style.

Herb-Marinated Barbequed Duck

MAKES ENOUGH
MARINADE FOR ONE
QUARTERED DUCK, TO
SERVE 2–4

6 tablespoons chopped mixed
fresh herbs (basil,
thyme, sage)
½ cup white wine vinegar
½ cup olive oil
¼ teaspoon ground
black pepper
1 shallot, peeled and sliced
2 cloves garlic, sliced

1   Combine all the ingredients thoroughly. Marinate the duck overnight.

2   Remove the duck from the marinade and barbeque according to one of the methods on page 157. Baste with the marinade occasionally.

LAGNIAPPE

Lagniappe, "a little something extra" . . . . These, then, are recipes that can be used to embellish a wide range of other dishes. Although each one will involve duck in some fashion, their use is not limited to the context of a duck presentation. These recipes should serve to free your sense of culinary creativity and expand your repertoire for imaginative uses of duck.

Duck Ham

MAKES 2 BREAST HAMS

1 whole Moulard duck breast
1½ cups kosher salt
Red wine vinegar
Ground white pepper

This recipe comes from Ariane Daguin of D'Artagnan, Inc. (see Sources, page 179), a native of Gascony, where duck and geese are king. The duck breast is cured as you would a ham, hence the name. It is good thinly sliced over wild greens, used as an hors d'oeuvre, or as an ingredient or seasoning in another dish. There is some controversy about the safety of eating uncooked duck meat, but it has been prepared and consumed this way for generations.

1   Divide the duck breast in half. Score the skin of each half, making square patterns, but do not cut all the way through to the meat.

2   Bury the breasts in the salt and refrigerate overnight.

3   Use the red wine vinegar to quickly rinse off the salt. Do not use water as this will cause the meat to regain some of the moisture it lost in the curing.

4   Cover generously on all sides with ground pepper. Wrap each half well in cheesecloth and tie the ends closed with twine. Hang in a cool, dry place, such as a basement, for about 15 days. The duck will feel much firmer when it is properly cured.

5   When ready, remove the cheesecloth and refrigerate the meat, well wrapped.

Curing duck meat in this manner withdraws much of its moisture and ultimately alters the relationship that it will have with wine. Its affinity with various wines is improved, although when used as a seasoning, it is the other elements in the dish that are likely to be of more concern.

For instance, thinly sliced duck ham over a wild green salad would pair delightfully with a crisp, dry rosé; however, in the stuffing of a roast duck, its lightly salted presence will not be the determining factor in the choice of wine.

Mandarin Pigeon

Mandarin Pancakes

MAKES APPROXIMATELY 10 PANCAKES

1 cup flour, sifted
Pinch of kosher salt
½ cup boiling water
Sesame oil for brushing

These pancakes are also known as Peking duck or moo shu pancakes. Commercial ones can be bought at some Chinese markets, but they are much better made at home. They can be made ahead and refrigerated or frozen and then steamed in foil to reheat. The technique of rolling out two pieces of sandwiched dough gives you two extra-thin pancakes after they are cooked and finally separated. Be careful not to brown them too quickly —they must remain pliable enough to wrap around the duck.

1   Place the flour and salt in a bowl and make a well. Add the water all at once. Stir with a spoon to combine until the dough is cool enough to handle.

2   Knead on a lightly floured board for about 10 minutes, until the dough is smooth and elastic. Cover loosely with plastic wrap and let rest for 20 minutes.

3   Roll out the dough on a lightly floured board to about ¼-inch thick. Cut out 3-inch circles.

4   Brush half the circles with sesame oil then place the remaining unoiled circles on top of these. Let rest, covered with plastic wrap, for 10 minutes.

5   Roll out the sandwiched circles very thin, to about 6 inches in diameter.

6 Heat a 10-inch skillet. Lightly brush both sides of each pancake with sesame oil as you are about to cook it. Cook one at a
time in the dry skillet. The pancake will get speckled and puff.
Turn and brown the other side. It should take about 30 seconds
to cook each side.

7 Remove to a plate and keep the pancakes covered so they
won't dry out. Separate the sandwiched pancakes as soon as you
can handle them, and stack. Wrap the stack in foil if not serving
immediately. These can be served wrapped in a tea towel to
retain moisture and heat.

New Potatoes with Duck Fat and Garlic

SERVES 2

12 small new potatoes, of uniform size

2 tablespoons rendered duck fat, melted

1 teaspoon kosher salt

½ teaspoon ground black pepper

2 teaspoons finely chopped garlic

For optimum browning, roast these potatoes in a preheated cast iron skillet.

1   Quarter the new potatoes.

2   In a bowl, combine the potatoes with the rest of the ingredients and mix thoroughly.

3   Roast in a 400° oven for about 40 minutes, stirring occasionally, until the potatoes are nicely browned.

Garlic Confit

Garlic lovers will find this canapé an absolute delight. Serve the sweet, soft garlic smashed onto soft toasts, or as a garnish for anything from fish to lamb.

1   Separate the head of garlic into cloves and peel carefully, leaving the cloves intact.

2   Combine in a bowl with the spices and salt. Marinate in the refrigerator for 24 hours.

3   Melt the duck fat in a small pot. Rinse the garlic and add it to the fat. Gently cook the garlic at just below a simmer for 30–45 minutes, until soft. Serve immediately or store in a glass or ceramic container, covered by the duck fat. This keeps indefinitely. Be sure to serve the garlic confit warm, heated in a little duck fat.

The euphoria created from the unabashed consumption of garlic confit requires no further mind-, body-, or emotion-altering substances.

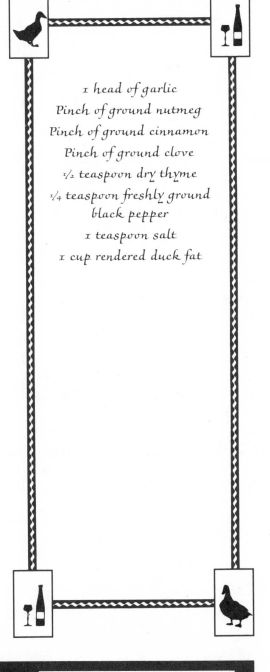

1 head of garlic
Pinch of ground nutmeg
Pinch of ground cinnamon
Pinch of ground clove
1/2 teaspoon dry thyme
1/4 teaspoon freshly ground
black pepper
1 teaspoon salt
1 cup rendered duck fat

Duck Focaccia

MAKES
ONE LOAF,
ABOUT 12 X 16 INCHES

3½ teaspoons active dry yeast

1½ cups warm water,
about 110°

1 teaspoon sugar

8 tablespoons melted duck fat

3¾–4 cups bread flour

1½ teaspoons salt

2 teaspoons chopped
rosemary

½ teaspoon freshly ground
black pepper

Duck fat and sesame oil for
greasing

This rustic bread was developed by Mark Hellerman, a chef and culinary arts instructor in New York City. It can be topped with cracklings, olives, more herbs, garlic, onions, and the like. It makes a great snack to go with before-dinner drinks or with the meal itself.

1   Combine the yeast, water, sugar, and 5 tablespoons of the melted duck fat in a bowl and stir to dissolve the yeast. Let rest, covered with a towel, for 5–10 minutes, until the yeast foams.

2   Combine the flour with ½ teaspoon of the salt, the rosemary, and pepper, and gradually add it to the yeast mixture, first stirring with a spoon and then with your hand as it gets too stiff. Turn the dough out onto a floured surface and knead for about 10 minutes, until you have a smooth, elastic ball.

3   Place the dough in a large greased bowl, cover with plastic wrap, and refrigerate overnight. The dough will rise very slowly this way, giving it a good flavor and texture.

4   Remove the bowl from the refrigerator and let the dough come to room temperature for about one hour.

5   Generously grease a 12- x 16-inch sheet pan with some sesame oil and duck fat, using mostly duck fat. Press the dough onto the sheet pan with your fingertips so you make little indentations as you are doing it. Brush the top with the remaining 3 tablespoons melted duck fat and sprinkle with the remaining salt.

6   Bake in a preheated 450° oven for 20–25 minutes, until the bread is nicely browned.

Cornbread

1   Combine and sift the dry ingredients.

2   Combine the melted butter and honey and cool to room temperature.

3   Combine the butter and honey with the eggs and milk. Add the liquids all at once to the dry ingredients and stir just enough to combine.

4   Bake in a greased 9- x 9-inch baking pan at 425° for 20 minutes, or until a skewer inserted into the center comes out clean.

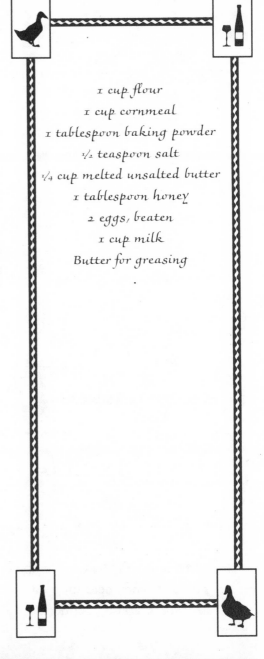

1 cup flour
1 cup cornmeal
1 tablespoon baking powder
1/2 teaspoon salt
1/4 cup melted unsalted butter
1 tablespoon honey
2 eggs, beaten
1 cup milk
Butter for greasing

Crackling Biscuits

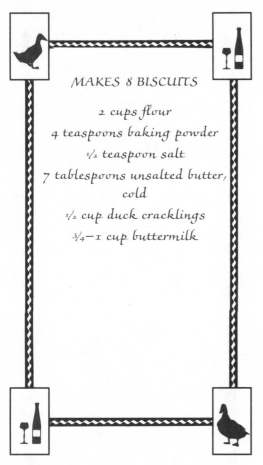

MAKES 8 BISCUITS

2 cups flour

4 teaspoons baking powder

1/2 teaspoon salt

7 tablespoons unsalted butter, cold

1/2 cup duck cracklings

3/4–1 cup buttermilk

1   Sift the dry ingredients together and place in a bowl.

2   Cut in the butter until it is the size of peas.

3   Add the duck cracklings (see Rendering Duck Fat page 26) and stir to distribute them evenly.

4   Add enough buttermilk just to moisten the flour and mix until just combined. Gather the biscuit dough into a ball and place it on a floured surface.

5   Sprinkle the dough with flour and roll it out to ½-inch thick. Cut out squares or circles and place them on a buttered sheet pan. Brush the tops with either melted butter or a little buttermilk egg wash.

6   Bake in a preheated 400° oven for about 15 minutes, until lightly browned.

Duck Fat Spreads

Duck fat may be used as a spread for bread. It is similar to schmaltz (chicken fat), and has significantly less cholesterol and saturated fat than butter. You can be creative with added flavorings, using shallots, herbs, chopped olives, wine, garlic, or nuts, for example. Have the duck fat at room temperature, combine it with whatever ingredients you wish, then refrigerate it, letting the flavors meld for a day or two. You may have trouble convincing skeptics of the actual benefits of consuming duck fat in this way as an alternative to butter, but they will love the taste!

Duck Blood

Duck blood is tricky to find because stringent USDA regulations make it almost impossible for a farmer to collect. Should you be lucky enough to come across some, there are lots of delicious possibilities for its use. When heated, the duck blood coagulates, holding together like a cake, and it has a delicate, though distinctly livery taste. You can sauté it with garlic and herbs as the French do, or stir-fry it with curry as is done in Malaysia. It can also be combined in its liquid state with bread and mushrooms, grains, or chopped greens, and used to fill sausage casings, in which case it is known as black sausage or blood pudding. Small amounts of blood are also used by Europeans to thicken sauces and soups.

Duck Eggs

Duck eggs can be found in many forms. The fresh ones are most commonly seen as your everyday unfertilized brown or white eggs and can be used in the same way you would chicken eggs, except that they won't form as good a meringue. Sometimes when you are buying duck eggs, at a farmers' market perhaps, you will be cautioned to watch out for the little bones. In this case you have found the little-known or -appreciated fertilized duck eggs, with the egg just beginning to develop into a duckling. Chinese markets will supply you with duck eggs in various preserved forms, the salted version of which is used as a seasoning. The well-known thousand-year egg is made by burying duck eggs in a clay solution for several months, which causes the raw egg to become firm like a cooked one and to turn a beautiful greenish blue color. This is eaten alone, as an appetizer, at a special meal.

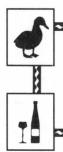

Sources

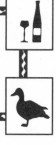

COMMONWEALTH FARMS
P.O. Box 449
Mongaup Valley, New York 12762
(914) 583-6630

Producers of fresh Moulard foie gras, Moulard duck, and duck parts.

CRESCENT DUCK PROCESSING CO.
P.O. Box 500
Edgar Avenue
Aquebogue, Long Island, New York 11931
(516) 722-8000

Producers of fresh and frozen Pekin duck, fully dressed or in Buddhist or Confucian styles.

D'ARTAGNAN, INC.
399 St. Paul Avenue
Jersey City, New Jersey 07306
(201) DAR-TAGN

Purveyors of a wide variety of game, including several breeds of duck, Moulard foie gras, and various duck products.

FOGGY RIDGE GAMEBIRD FARM
P.O. Box 211
Warren, Maine 04864
(207) 273-2357

Producers of a variety of game birds, including fresh Mallard ducks in season.

THE GAME EXCHANGE
P.O. Box 880204
San Francisco, California 94188
(800) 426-3872

Suppliers of Pekin, Muscovy, and Rouen ducks as well as a variety of farm-raised game birds.

GRIMAUD FARMS OF CALIFORNIA, INC.
11665 N. Clements Road
Linden, California 95236
(209) 887-3121

Producers of Muscovy ducks.

REICHART DUCK FARMS
3770 Middle Two Rock Road
Petaluma, California 94952
(707) 762-6314

Producers of fresh and frozen Pekin duck, fully dressed or in Buddhist or Confucian styles.

SONOMA FOIE GRAS
P.O. Box 2007
Sonoma, California 95476
(707) 938-0496

Producers of fresh Muscovy foie gras.

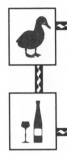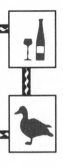

Bibliography

Chang, K.C., ed. *Food in Chinese Culture.* New Haven: Yale University Press, 1977.

Composition of Foods, Raw-Processed-Prepared. U.S. Department of Agriculture, Agricultural Research Service Handbook No. 8. Washington, D.C.: U.S. Government Printing Office, 1978–89.

Daguin, André, and Anne de Ravel. *Foie Gras, Magret, and Other Good Food from Gascony.* New York: Random House, 1988.

Editors of *Countryside Magazine. Raising Animals for Fun and Profit.* Tab Books, 1984.

Fortino, Denise. "Why French Hearts Fare Well." *Food and Wine,* 1990, p. 136.

Jull, Morley A. *Raising Turkeys, Ducks, Geese and Game Birds.* New York: McGraw-Hill Book Co., 1947.

Kellam, Susan. "Farmers Rallying to Uphold L.I. Duck Heritage." *The New York Times,* October 30, 1983, Long Island Weekly section, p. 1.

Knudson, Thomas J. "Duck Growers on L.I. Dwindling, Under Pressures of Costs and Suburbia." *The New York Times,* January 10, 1986, Metropolitan section, p. 1.

Lamon, Harry M., and Rob R. Slocum. *Ducks and Geese.* New York: Orange Judd Publishing Co., 1922.

McGee, Harold. *On Food and Cooking, The Science and Lore of the Kitchen.* New York: Collier Books, Macmillan Publishing Co., 1984.

Phillips, John. *A Natural History of the Ducks.* New York: Dover Publications, 1986.

Raethel, Heinz-Sigurd. *The New Duck Handbook*. New York: Barron's Educational Series, 1989.

Reliable Poultry Journal Publishing Company. *Ducks and Geese*. Quincy, Illinois, 1910.

Steingarten, Jeffrey. "Why Aren't the French Dropping Like Flies?" *Notable News, Vogue*, February 1991, p. 248.

U.S. Department of Agriculture. *Agricultural Statistics*. Washington, D.C.: U.S. Government Printing Office, 1960–87.

Index

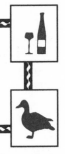